The Truth About Stress:

Understanding Your Life
From The Inside Out

Richard Flint

Copyright 2004

ISBN# 0-937851-32-9

Printed in the United States of America.
For information, address Flint, Inc.,
11835 Canon Blvd., Suite C-105,
Newport News, VA 23606-2570
1-800-368-8255

www.RichardFlint.com

First edition, 1982
Second edition, 1983
Third edition, 1984
Fourth edition, 1987
Fifth edition, 2001
Sixth edition, 2004

DEDICATION

*To Janet Sparks whose presence in my
life was a gift that I shall cherish as
long as I have a breath to take.*

*Thank You Janet for your love of
people and your love for life.*

I miss your smile!

Table of Contents

PREFACE
A Personal Message From Richard Flint For You

There has always been stress for humans to deal with, *but* most people have just accepted it as an ever-present part of life. They have laughed when their attention was called to it and joked about that this stress is going to kill me. 9/11 changed all that!

Here we were, a nation that felt invincible to the events the rest of the world was facing. Here we were, secure in our country, living our daily lives without any fear of the evil things that were happening "over there." Here we were, fat, comfortable, smug and enjoying the "lifestyle" most of the world couldn't fathom.

Then, it happened! In a few moments that changed the course of our country, our little secure, smug, invincible world was awakened. With the actions of a few people everything we thought couldn't happen, happened. No longer were we a nation unto ourselves; no longer were we a nation protected from the evils the rest of the world were struggling with; no longer were we calm, cool and collected. Now, with the events of a brief space in time, our little secure world was redesigned.

Our calmness was replaced with fear; our little secure corners of life were filled with "what's next." The feeling we were untouchable was destroyed in the falling of two towers and the loss of over 3000 lives.

Since 9/11, we have become a different society. The fear created on the morning of 9/11 is still present; the "it won't happen here" attitude is constantly being restated with "what's next." The calmness of many people's lives has been weakened and for many their life has found worry, doubt and uncertainty to be their constant companions. We have become a nation that is wrestling with fear, shackled with worry, paralyzed by uncertainty and trapped by the unknown. The result of this has been an increase in people's personal stress.

When you take away a person's calmness, you increase their worry. The result will be an increase in their negative stress.

When you take away a person's clarity, you increase their personal doubt. That will result in an increase in their negative stress.

When you weaken a person's confidence, you increase their personal fear. The result will be an increase in their personal stress.

Never have I seen as much negative stress as I am seeing right now. Everyday I see it in the faces of people; I can hear it in the words they speak concerning their life; I can sense it in their behavior as they come face to face with decisions they need to make.

For many their faith has been shattered; their beliefs have been cracked and their spirit has been weakened. As much as they talk about "getting on with their life," they find themselves looking over their shoulder and questioning things they never questioned before. The result has been a new sense of personal tiredness, an unwillingness to reach too far into the future and a living pattern of cautious optimism.

The fear many found themselves wrestling with has also played havoc with the business sector. When fear grips people, their spending habits change. When worry grips a human life, spending habits are rethought. When people find themselves living with uncertainty, they tend to turn inward and become more conservative with their money. Put these together and the result became an economy that found itself reeling and uncertain what to do.

Look at how much money people lost in the stock market. The devastation of 9/11 became the devastation to many people's investments, retirement and lifestyle. Do you think that increased anyone's stress level?

Add 9/11 to what has happened through the unethical behavior of some of the so-called leaders in corporate America and the stress level accelerated. Who would have ever thought that those who were in-trusted with their life savings of their employees would allow greed to make it okay to steal from the people who invested their life in making the company successful.

Who would have ever thought that the desire for more would have over-shadowed the trust people had placed in leadership. How could those at the top justify destroying the life savings of those at the bottom? How evil do you have to be to make it okay to steal and then think you shouldn't be held accountable?

I think the stress people are dealing with today is as great as what people felt during the great depression. I believe the increase in stress over the past couple of years has awakened people to what their life isn't, what they have been avoiding, how unhappy they are with where they are and how lost they really are.

In the past couple of years, I have had more couples contact me about the instability in their relationships. It is not something that has just happened; it has been, but rather than them living with what the added stress has brought to their life, they want to face it and move beyond it. They are willing to take any step that is necessary.

In the past couple of years, I have had a huge increase in people wanting to talk to me about how unhappy they are in their careers. Yes, they have a job; yes, they have been going to it for years, but "no" they haven't been happy. Now, they want to cut themselves lose and see what their life can really be like. Look at the number of home based businesses that have been started; look at the number of people who have walked away from secure incomes and are willing to redesign their life in order to be happy. They want out of their stress trap; they see life as too short to stay where there is no happiness, no feeling of being valued and no sense of personal freedom. No longer are they willing to just hang out in an unappreciative environment where leadership is lining their pockets because of their hard work.

In the past few years look at how depression, anxiety, physical illness and other emotionally induced illness has taken over so many people's lives. The stress they had been bottling up has found an exit. The things they had become so attuned at avoiding could no longer be kept in their personal hiding closet. The negative side of stress had raised its ugly head and taken over the emotional aspect of people's lives.

You need this book! You need to slow down and make this book part of your journey of personal understanding. This is not a book about getting rid of your stress; if you do that, you will be dead. This is a book about learning the truth about stress. It is not an emotional game book, a magical book, or a book that holds all the answers. What it is is a guidebook that will help you CONTROL the stress in your life. What this book is, is an emotional friend that can be called upon when you feel your life is out of control, and you are trapped in the darkness of confusion. It is sensitive to what you are going through; it is truthful about why you are there, and it is revealing about what you need to do to get away from the negative side of stress. It is about you, and it is written just for you!

CHAPTER 1
This Thing Called Stress

What is this thing called stress, anyway?

Have you ever had a day that was going great until you got out of bed? Have you ever awakened in the morning just knowing it was going to be a great day, only to have one telephone call, one memo, one client, one unexpected surprise, turn what *was* to be a great day into an arena filled with unwanted stress?

One Day of Unwanted Stress

Let me share with you a recent experience of a stress-filled day. It was just one of 133,623 *(but who counts them?)* I have had in the past few years from which I could draw an illustration.

Stress is: going to your travel agency, picking up an $8,000 airplane ticket, starting out on a seven-week speaking tour only to find out after two days on the road that the airline you're using has filed bankruptcy!

Each day I went to the airline ticket counter, filled with fear and anticipation, hoping the plane was there. If it was, I prayed that I could board. I did fine for three weeks and even made it to Peoria, Illinois.

I approached the ticket counter of Britt Airlines, where I was boarding for Chicago then connecting there for Roanoke, Virginia. As I put down my ticket, I noticed the alertness in the ticket agent's eyes. He stared at it and then said, *"Son, you've got a problem."*

1

I said, "What do you mean?"

"This ticket is written on Continental Airlines. They are in Chapter 11, and we are not honoring their tickets."

"Look," I said, as I thumbed through the portion that had already been used, "everybody else has taken them."

"We're not everybody else. They are in Chapter 11 and we are not honoring their tickets."

"But, I've got to get to Chicago! I have a connection. I've got to be in Roanoke tomorrow morning to speak for a convention."

"Well," he said, *"you are just going to have to purchase a ticket."*

"But, I've got a ticket."

"I can't take your ticket. If you are going to get to Chicago on this flight or any of our other flights, you are going to have to purchase a ticket."

Well, I didn't want to be intimidated, so I looked him square in the eye and said with authority, "Let me speak to your supervisor."

He looked me square in the eye with the same authority and said, *"What do you want to say to me?"*

"How do I get to Chicago?"

"You purchase a ticket," was his reply.

Five minutes later, I was purchasing a ticket. I made it to Chicago and ran to my connecting gate.

Without even looking up, the attendant at the gate said, *"Did you run all the way across the airport?"*

As I lay stretched across her counter, gasping for a breath of air, she looked up at me and responded, *"You didn't have to run."*

"Why?" I asked, but not really wanting her to answer—I

knew what was coming next.

"Because your plane has been canceled."

"Canceled!" I said with a low roar, trying to contain my frustration. "What do you mean, 'canceled'?"

"That means the plane is not going to fly."

"Why was it canceled?"

"Mechanical problem."

There is one thing that is certain about traveling by air: you DON'T want to take a plane with mechanical problems!

"Okay. When is your next available flight to Roanoke?"

"We can get you there at 2:30 p.m. tomorrow."

"That's no good. I have to speak at 8:30 a.m. tomorrow."

"I'm sorry. That's the best I can do"

What about another airline? Can you check for me?

"I don't have time right now to check."

"Your airline causes me this problem and now you don't have time to try to help me?"

"I'm really busy."

"Too busy to help me? You are a service representative for this airline. This airline has created a problem for me. Now we are going to see what you and your airline can do to remedy the situation."

Realizing that I was serious, she threw down her pen, looked at me and said, *"Let me see what I can do."*

After what seemed like hours checking her computer, she said, *"Okay, I've got it worked out. Here is what we are going to do. We are going to take you over to United Airlines, put you on their flight and fly you to Greensboro, North Carolina. There, we will put you in a van and drive you to Roanoke."*

"What time do I get there?"

3

"You will arrive in Roanoke at 5:28 a.m. tomorrow."

"Okay, just one more question: What about my luggage?"

"Don't worry," she said, *"we will take care of it."*

"Oh, no." I said. "Another airline told me that, and they are *still* taking care of it. I'm not leaving until I get three baggage checks that show me my luggage has been rerouted to go with me."

After she reluctantly gave me the claim checks, I thanked her for her help and headed for the United Airlines counter.

I arrived in Greensboro and found the baggage claim area. The attendant saw me searching for my bags. *"Are you looking for three pieces of luggage?"*

I looked at him with a shocking stare.

"I'll bet you're wondering how I knew that?"

Without saying a word, I just shook my head "yes."

"I have a message here from Piedmont Airlines telling me to tell you, when you arrived, to go ahead and get into the van and go to Roanoke. When you get to Roanoke, go to the airport and pick up your luggage."

I wondered, "Why could my luggage get there and I couldn't?"

I said, "You mean my luggage is in Roanoke?"

"That's what this message says."

"May I have that piece of paper?"

I took the paper, got into the van and headed for Roanoke. At 5:36 a.m., we pulled up in front of the Roanoke airport. I jumped out and went in to find the baggage service agent for Piedmont Airlines.

I said, "Hi. My name is Richard Flint..." and I explained the saga.

With a look of bewilderment on his face, he said, *"I don't have your luggage. We haven't had any flights in here from Chicago."*

"That's okay. You find my luggage. I'm going to the hotel and going to bed."

An hour later my phone rang in the hotel. I heard a voice at the other end say: *"Hey, I found your luggage."*

"Great, where is it?

"Chicago. It will be here at 2:30 p.m. today."

Okay. I've dealt with this before. No time to go shopping, so I had to do my program in the same clothes I had on for the past day and a half. At least I was in the right location!

I went to the front desk of the hotel and inquired about the boxes that my office had sent for the program.

"Oh, you need to talk to the catering manager."

After following her directions I found the catering manager.

"My name is Richard Flint..."

"And you're looking for seven boxes."

"Yes, and that must mean you have them."

"Well," he said, *"I have good news and bad news. The good news is that the boxes are here in Roanoke. The bad news is that the hotel is on strike and UPS will not cross the picket line. Your boxes are in town, but they are down at the UPS office."*

"That's no problem," I said, "Just send someone there to get them."

"None of my people will go."

"Then you go. I really need those boxes."

"You don't understand. I'm the catering manager and I don't do things like that anymore. That is not my job."

5

"Okay," I said. "Let's you and me go find the general manager's office and talk to him about this situation."

After a long pause, he said, *"It will take me about forty-five minutes to get there and back. Now, where would you like those boxes delivered?"*

Stress is your constant companion,
but that doesn't have to be a bad thing!

Stress is here to stay. When you understand what stress is, you understand that you do not go through a single day without it. It is an everyday part of your life. So, what do you do with it? Do you manage *it*, or does it manage *you*? Do you try to understand it, or do you just accept it and let it have its way?

You must understand that stress is not only an everyday part of your life, but also a normal part of your life. Each day, in many different ways, you experience it. Each day, with the things that need to be done, the things that don't get done, phone calls, dealing with other people and unexpected events, you encounter stress.

Have you ever had a day when you wanted to throw everything on the floor and run away? Have you ever been upset because there never seems to be any time for you? People always want to know if you have time for them. Don't they ever consider or understand that you need time for yourself?

Stress is your constant companion everyday of your life. What do you do? There seems to be no stopping it. Things just seem to spin faster and faster. The pressure builds and builds until you feel you are slipping into the danger zone. That little voice inside of you begins to scream, "Warning! Warning! You are about to explode! You must do something! Warning! Your life is about to disintegrate!" Yet, the more you try to turn your pressure valve down, the more the pressure seems to build. What do you do? Can you stop it? Some of your friends tell you that it's something you have to live with as a normal part of life: just forget about trying to control it and move on. This philosophy sets you up to one-day find yourself out of control and without a life.

Listen closely: This philosophy is dangerously wrong. You will never completely remove stress from your life, and truthfully, you don't want to. Certain aspects of stress are healthy. Some stress is actually good for you!

The secret is learning to control *your* stress in your life.

The Truth

Here is the truth that is the nerve center of this book: *People who work to eliminate stress become stressful. People who learn to control stress become creative.* That's right. Stress is fertile ground for creativity. Don't you accomplish more when the pressure is on *and* you are in control? Stress is your friend when you let it be your friend. It is only your enemy when you fight with it.

The more you understand about this thing called stress, and the more you understand about yourself, the better you will be at controlling your stress in your life. The plan isn't to eliminate stress; it is to learn to control it in your everyday life — not just when catastrophes happen. This cannot be achieved without understanding what stress is, what it is not, and what it can and will do to your life.

7

A Definition

What is this thing called stress? We read about it, hear about it and talk about it. Stress has become a fact of life that draws attention to itself from every corner of society. The term "stress" isn't really new. It was created slightly over sixty years ago by a young doctor named Hans Selye.[1]

Can you imagine what people called this stuff in our lives before there ever was a term for it? It is one of those words that is all encompassing and many people don't have a clue what stress really means to them. Sometimes to understand what something *is*, you must first learn what it *is NOT*.

What Stress Is NOT

First, stress is not simply nervous tension. Experiments have shown that plants and animals can even have nervous tension. Stress for us is way deeper than that.

Second, stress is not an emergency discharge of hormones or adrenaline. I know you have heard the stories of people doing superhuman feats because of an "adrenaline charge." Some people think this is stress. The reaction maybe a result of stress, but it is not stress itself.

Third, stress does not always result in some sort of damage. You can have a stressful game of tennis or drive to work without damaging your body.

Stress is not vague to our lives, like we may wish it to be. Stress is very specific. It affects certain organs in a highly selective manner. This is how God works your little "whispers" that are really warning signs to get your attention.

Stress does not create stress. We may think that stress just keeps producing more stress. That's not exactly true. Your stress is actually caused by a specific agent of stress called a stressor. Now don't get too concerned about the technical terms. The two things you need to get from this book are:

1. Understanding what your stress is.
2. Knowing where it comes from so you can learn to control it.

Stress should not be avoided. Stop and think about this: you would have to literally be dead in order to NOT have any stress.

The most practical definition of stress, and the one we will use for this book, is this: **Stress is anything in life that makes you uptight.**

So, now we know that it can happen any time and anywhere. If it's so "natural" then why should you worry about it? Shouldn't you just accept it and go on with living your life? The answer is a profound yes and an equally profound no!

Yes, you must go on with living your life. You know stress is going to be a part of everyday you live. If you spend all your time worrying about it, you will become a stressful mess. You will only create more stress.

No, you cannot afford to pretend it does not exist. The effect it can have on you is far too great to just close your eyes and pretend it does not exist. You must recognize its presence in your life. When you do this, you'll find that stress becomes your friend. If you don't do this, stress becomes a time bomb that ticks each day until it explodes. Then, it has become the worst kind of enemy.

It is important you understand that stress will not confine itself to one area of your life. Have you ever had something at work make you uptight, and rather than handling it at work, you brought it home with you? Have you ever had a little disagreement at home, and rather than handling it there, you took it to work? Have you ever been upset because you could not find time for yourself, and barked at someone else? You must realize that pressure in any one area of your life will always find its way into the other areas.

The next chapters are designed to help you understand your stress. Your life is like a four-room house. Each room holds its own unique stress. The stress in each room has a tremendous effect on the rest of your house. The more you understand the stress in each room, the better prepared you will be to deal with the affect on your life. Read these chapters with an open mind.

These words are filled with truths you need to understand in order to grasp the truth about stress.

Before you move on, take a short quiz. This **Stress Quiz**[2] is designed to help you determine the level of stress in your daily life.

Instructions:
Only check those events, which have occurred within the last twelve months. For each yes answer, give yourself one point. Then add up your total score. The answer key is at the end of the test. Have fun and be honest.

THE STRESS QUIZ[2]

1. Have you been drinking, smoking or eating more than usual?   Yes   No

2. Do you have difficulty sleeping at night?   Yes   No

3. Are you more grouchy and argumentative than usual?   Yes   No

4. Do you have trouble with your boss?   Yes   No

5. Did you or a loved one experience a serious illness?   Yes   No

6. Have you recently divorced?   Yes   No

7. Has there been an increase in the number of marital or family arguments?   Yes   No

8. Have you been experiencing sexual difficulties?   Yes   No

9. Did a close relative or friend die?   Yes   No

10. Did you marry or recently start living with someone?   Yes   No

THE STRESS QUIZ

11. Has there been a pregnancy or birth in your family?   Yes   No

12. Do you have financial problems?   Yes   No

13. Did you get fired or change jobs?   Yes   No

14. Do you feel jumpy and on edge, flying off the handle at little things?   Yes   No

15. Do you watch television more than three hours a day?   Yes   No

16. Have you had trouble with the IRS or the law?   Yes   No

17. Has there been an increase in the number of deadlines or work hours?   Yes   No

18. Have you moved or changed residence?   Yes   No

19. Do you have trouble with your in-laws?   Yes   No

20. Are you exposed to constant noise at home or work?   Yes   No

ANSWER KEY

1-5   Stress is not likely to cause any problems.

6-10   Stress is moderate and will not harm you if you watch your diet and get rest.

11-15   Try to reduce some of the stress in your life or you risk suffering poor health.

16-20   Stress is excessive and may make you susceptible to a major illness.[2]

CHAPTER 2
The Stress Module

Stress is "anything in life that makes you uptight." That definition makes stress an all-inclusive part of your life. It can be anything at any time or at any place. Anything that takes you out of your comfortable routine will create pressure, which you must deal with in some way.

Stress is anything in life
that makes you uptight.

I remember the first blind date I ever had. I was sixteen, shy, and not experienced in the dating world. My best friend was Mike. We did everything together. Mike's girlfriend was Robin. She lived in a neighboring town and went to a different school. Her school was having a dance, and Robin wanted me to take her best friend. I really did not want any part of this, but Mike kept after me until I finally said "yes."

You talk about uptight! I was a nervous wreck. When I'm nervous, I can't be still. For days, I was nothing but nervous energy. I called that date off a thousand times in my mind.

Finally, the day arrived. I was more than uptight. I was scared to death! The time came for Robin and Mike to pick me up so we could go get Sharon. All the way to Sharon's house, they kept telling me how nice she was and how much fun we would have.

There we were, in front of her house. All I remember was Mike pulling me out of the car and pushing me toward

15

the front door. When I arrived at the door, my hand would not reach for the doorbell. She must have known I was there. The door opened and there stood this gorgeous giant. She must have been seven feet tall!

Now, I have always had this rule: I do not date women who are taller than I am.

I remember looking up at her and saying, "Wow, you're tall!" I then turned and started walking home. That was the first and last blind date I ever had.

Stress is: anything in life that makes you uptight. Anything that creates a redirection or a different perspective or takes you out of your routine creates pressure.

Remember the philosophy that forms the nerve center of this book: People who work to eliminate stress become stressful. People who learn to control stress become creative.

To control stress, you must understand how stress is created in your own life. The more you understand the process, the better you will be at controlling the pressure.

Sometimes it's easier for us to understand how something works when we can see all the parts in motion. Here's a diagram of how stress is created in your life:[3]

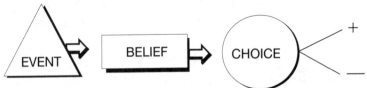

Each day is filled with events. Nothing happens during your day that does not fit into the total of that day's events. An event can take the form of someone or something. Other people do not have to be present for you to experience the event. These events can be outside or inside of you.

Your outside events, those involving other people, are much easier to identify. People create visual and tangible situations. These are much easier to understand.

The internal events are far more difficult to handle. Most of us are visual. What you can see or touch you find much easier to work with in a constructive fashion. When you are dealing with an intangible, it becomes more challenging. An internal event may be a thought, a pain, or a feeling. To describe a pain is much more difficult than to describe a person who is a pain!

The important point to realize is everyday is made up of events. When your day is over, you will process it through your events.

With each event, you have a feeling about what that event means to your life. That feeling is your opinion that defines the event. Have you ever seen two people go through the same situation and emerge with two different opinions as to what the event meant to them? People may share common events, but develop different meanings because of their unique feelings.

Opinions are the emotions that you bring to, and take away from, the events. The key to understanding the events is understanding the opinions you have AND what created those feelings.

Events trigger feelings and you make a choice based on your beliefs. The choice is your visual response to the events.

The event is the situation; the feeling is the emotion; the choice is the response.

Some people feel they have no choices. The way they deal with every event is based upon a feeling that is seen as the response. This is important to know: *there is no such thing as having no choice.*

17

If an event is interpreted as pleasant, happy, welcome, nonthreatening, familiar, and wholesome, you will choose to respond with a positive action. If the response you choose is negative and stressful, you will experience some kind of alarm from your internal system. If you resist and persist in your behavior, your resistance will grow to the point of total frustration. That frustration will cause a breakdown in your system if you do not deal with it in a way where you completely understand what's going on.

Dr. Barbara Brown describes a seven-step process that we go through each time we make negative decisions about events in our lives.[4]

1. **Expectation**. The reaction to an event starts with an expectation of what the event will be like.

2. **Distress**. This step has to do with your perceptions of the events in your life.

3. **The Worry Mode**. This step is when your mind goes into a problem-solving posture.

4. **Uncertainty**. As you try to figure out the solution to your problem, you may ask whether or not the solution will work. You may realize that you really don't have control over the future outcome and may begin to immobilize yourself with resistance to change.

5. **Expansive Images of Worry**. Your mind will remember all the past events that were similar to this present event and will seek for some solace in this quickening tension.

6. **Contemplation.** In this step, the circuits of the mind begin to close and the only thing which gains your attention is the unsolved problem, the uncertain future, and the uneasy feelings of tension, fear and stress.

7. **Self-destruction.** This is the final step.

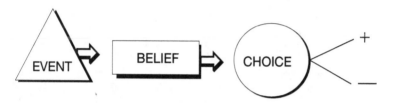

This module is vital if you are to understand how stress is created in your life. The key is to understand in which sphere the stress actually happens. There are three theories here.

The first theory believes the stress occurs in the event. When the event first happens, the stress exists. This doesn't make sense to me. The event is the stressor, not the stress.

Another school says the stress occurs with the choice. When the choice has been made, the stress exists. I cannot agree with that either. The choice is the aftermath of the whole situation. Stress does not happen after-the-fact.

I believe stress is created with the feeling. You can only understand an event through your feelings. The feelings are the emotions that create the response. That gives definition to the stress.

Keep the above module in mind as you read on. It will become your reference point when you are unclear about a stress creator in the different areas of your life.

19

CHAPTER 3
Your Four-Room House

Let's look at your life as a house that you live in so you'll understand the main areas of your life and how stress affects those areas.

Life is more than just one giant room you live in each day. Life is a house you spend your time and energy arranging and roaming through. This is not your ordinary house. You spend each and everyday of your life decorating, arranging, redecorating, and rearranging with your presence.

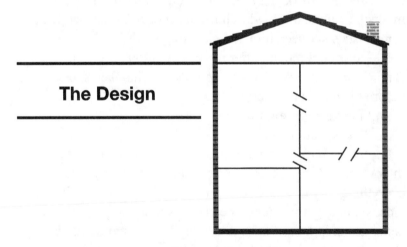

The Design

This is a unique house because it contains four very important rooms. It is interesting to watch these rooms take size and shape. In the beginning they are neither constant in their size or their shape. Neither are they constant in their importance. Then, as you begin to grow and establish priorities, your house takes on a very definite size and shape. At this time, the rooms become very definable.

The Business Room

The first room is the business or professional room. This is the largest room in your house. It is the room that supplies the financial security for the rest of the house. The stress in this room comes in a variety of forms. The stress here creates the largest arena of mental pressure all occupants have to handle in their daily pattern of existence. This room is constantly in conflict with the family and personal rooms. Let's see if this sounds familiar to you:

Mark is young, talented and driven to be #1 in his company. He works a lot of hours and comes home most nights late and exhausted. This pattern of behavior had led to some issues between him and his wife, Sandra.

He sought me out after my presentation on "Achieving Balance In Your Life." As he approached, his face spoke before his mouth even came open.

"I have a question for you."

"Okay, shoot."

"Do you really think it is possible to achieve balance in your life? I mean there never seems to be enough time for everything. I work hard in order to provide for my wife and kids, yet all I get when I come home is more crap about not being around. Doesn't she understand why I am doing this?"

"NO! All she understands is that you are not there. I would bet she appreciates all you are doing, but your absence creates stress for her which she hands to you."

"Stress! She doesn't know stress. I am yanked and pulled each and everyday at work. There is no time for me and half the things I need to do. I have to do this! All I want from her is a little consideration for all I am doing."

"Mark, put yourself in her shoes. She is home all day with the kids. She looks forward to your coming home, only to have you arrive worn out and with very little patience for her or the kids. If there is not balance between the business and family rooms, there will always be conflict."

The Family Room

The second largest room in your house is the family room. This is the room you most constantly share with the other people who are very important to your life. The stress here is as great as that in the business room, but often the pressure is more difficult to deal with because it is more emotional than mental. In today's society, the pressure is different than it was twenty-five years ago. With the increase in the divorce rate, this room has had to expand to deal with the yours-mine-and-ours family. People who have shared the family room with you never completely move out of it. They may not be as visible as they once were, but they will always maintain a closet where some of their emotional effects can be found. That one fact can make this a very stressful room. This room stays in constant conflict with the business room, the personal room, and on some occasions, the social room.

Mike and Patty have been married for ten years. They have a happy, but stressful marriage. In order to maintain the lifestyle they want, they both have to work. Both of their jobs are demanding and exhausting. Add to that the fact they have three children who cling to them each evening.

At least two evenings a week either Mike or Patty are gone to meetings. That means the one left home has to take care of everything. As much as they each love their children,

23

they feel the stress of being one of the millions of "stretched families."

I had finished my program one night and was gathering my things when I saw them charging toward me.

I stepped back and in a half joking way asked, "Are you after me?"

They stopped dead in their tracks, looked at each other and laughed. "I guess we appear that way," Mike said with a big grin on his face.

"We're sorry. If you are busy, we can talk to you later," Patty said with this look on her face that was begging for time with me.

"No, I'm okay right now. Let's go find a place and talk."

We found a quiet corner and for the next hour I listened as they described their out-of-control life.

Patty looked at me and said, "Are we the most messed up couple you have ever seen?"

I smiled, leaned forward and replied, "No! In fact, you are pretty normal. Listen you two; you are just too stretched. You don't have time for family and it is driving both of you crazy. You both come from homes where family time was important, but you have designed your lives so there is no time for family. You have got to slow your rat race down and find time to satisfy this emotional need before it destroys the two of you and your kids. Remember, what they will know about family will be defined by what your behavior teaches them."

Their house was definitely out of sync. The collision that was happening between their business and family rooms was wearing out the entire family.

Joan is also typical of so many people in our society today. She is 31, the mother of two, career woman and a single parent.

I was in the meeting room packing my computer and projector when she wandered back in. I noticed her standing in the back of the room just staring at me. Having seen this behavior before, I knew she was waiting for permission to approach me.

"I bet you have a question for me."

That was all she needed to hear. She made her way to the front, sat down and for a moment and just looked at me. "I don't want to bother you."

"Hey, I've got to pack this stuff, so why not talk to you while I am doing it. I hope you don't mind if I continue to pack up while you talk."

"No, that's fine. I really felt that you were talking only to me tonight. You talk about a research case for stress — you are looking at it! My life is so overwhelming. My job is very time demanding; my kids are very emotionally demanding; my life is not a life. It is an existence. There are days I just want to stay in bed and hide under the covers, but then reality sets in. There are so many people who depend on me. Not just my kids, but my mom and my sister. They think I am the only one who can help them. I just don't have the energy to do it all. God, I just want to run away!"

We talked for over an hour about the confusion she was living in. We talked about creating time agendas for her and her children. The hardest conversation was about making her mother and sister responsible for their own lives.

"Joan, you have to put yourself on your own priority list. You have to arrange your stress house to have less stress, not more. As long as you allow everyone and everything else to have a greater presence than your family, you are going to be swallowed up in this guilt trip you have put on yourself. You

25

need to slow everything down and take control. It is very apparent you are being controlled, rather than taking control. All that does is feed your negative stress and continue to wear you down and at some point out."

Joan has a lot of emotional twins out there. There are millions of single parents who belong to the "stretched group." Their lives are not lives; they are a series of collisions that keep their family rooms in turmoil and crisis.

The Personal Room

The third room in your house is the personal room. This seems to be the one room that is in constant disarray. You have heard the saying, "In every house there is a junk room." Well, if your house is filled with a lot of stress, the personal room is the junk room. In this room, you tend to store all the garbage from all the other rooms. This room needs a lot of personal attention; yet, it seems to be the room you avoid the most. In most people's lives the personal room is the smallest of the four. This is a tragedy because this room needs to be the largest! It is from here you draw the strength needed to deal with the situations in the other rooms.

It is from spending time in your personal room that you learn about yourself. Lack of time spent in this room has a great effect on all the other rooms. There is not another room in the house that has as much importance to your life as this room. There is not another room in your house that can offer as much control as this room. There is not another room in your house that is as frightening as this room. Others will visit the personal room, but very few outsiders will understand your personal room. It is a private room viewed by, but seldom shared with, others.

Albert said it as well as anyone has ever said it to me. "Richard, I didn't realize how important my personal room was until I started using one. I am like so many who live their lives for others. I have always felt that time with me was not as important as time for others. Man, was I wrong! Since I have made my personal room a priority, my time with others has so much more meaning. As I have learned the importance of me, I discovered the value I bring to others. As long as I calm with me am I valuable to others. My personal room has brought me personal calmness. Thank you for introducing the idea and the need for time with me. Know what? I am learning to really enjoy being with me!"

The Social Room

The last of the four rooms is the social room. It is a very beneficial room if it is used for its intended purposes. This is the room for friends. This is the room for relaxation. This room is important because it is the room for social interchange. When used for the right reasons, this becomes a room where you can expand yourself through involvement with people, clubs, and organizations. Psychologically, the social room is your playroom. Its functioning smoothly is essential for good mental health.

Here's what is frightening about this room. Rather than being a room for growth, it has become a room for escape. Rather than being a room for relaxation, it has become a room of pressure. Rather than being a room for helping one's mental health, it has become a psychologically damaging room. This has become the number one room for escape. When the

27

pressure is too great in the business room, you often go to your social room to hide. When the pressure is too great in the family room, the social room has become the room for escape. When you avoid spending time alone in your personal room, the social room becomes your escape.

The social room is a room of strength and a room for growth when its purpose and position are kept in perspective. When this room becomes a room for escape, it becomes a very dangerous room in your house.

You live in a four-room house that can very appropriately be called The Stress House. There is absolutely nothing wrong with living in this house. Remember what we said in the very first chapter? Stress is a part of life. It is a fact, and there is no way of getting around it. If you try to avoid it, it will still get you. If you try to ignore its place in your life, it will still make its presence known. The secret is to understand the major causes of stress in each of the four rooms of your Stress House and to devise a plan to control those points of pressure.

People who work to eliminate
stress become stressful.
People who learn to control
stress become creative.

The choice is yours. You can take an honest look at each room, know the possibilities, and devise a plan of action; or you can close your eyes, pretend there is nothing to deal with in those rooms, and pay the cost brought on by avoiding it. Sure, the decision is something that can create stress, but stress is *anything in life that makes you uptight.*

Even if you choose not to deal with it, stress is still there and will make you uptight.

CHAPTER 4
Twelve Realities

Before you tour your Stress House, you need to stand in the front yard for a few minutes and take a look at some things that will make a difference to your tour. As you move through your Stress House, you are going to discover parts of your life in each room. As you sense and see this, you are going to ask "Why?" I'm going to give you twelve realities that will prepare you for your visit to your Stress House. Without an understanding of these twelve realities, you will enter the house without some very necessary information. These realities are not magical, but they give you insights you need to understand the truth about stress and control the stress in your life. You do not have to agree with what I say, but I do want you to pay close attention to what you are reading.

Reality 1:
You Create Your Own Realities

It is important that you understand this: *the only definition your mind has of "truth" is what you tell it.* The human mind records everything it sees and hears, but it only gives back what is requested.

Let's look at two people experiencing the same situation: one enters the situation, feels it is going to be bad, and spends his energy looking for the pain. He is really telling his mind, *"Show me the pain of this event."* What does his mind do? It shows him everything that is wrong and gives the requested pain. What is his mind doing? It is responding to his request.

Another person enters the same event, but asks her mind

31

to show the value of this situation in her life. What does her mind do? It shows the meaning and growth of the situation. What is her mind doing? It is giving the information requested.

Your mind responds to your request for information. It contains so much more than you ask, but it responds according to what you want.

The game Trivial Pursuit gives us a very valuable lesson. While playing the game, have you ever been asked a question you didn't think you knew the answer and had some strange thought pop into your mind? You blurted it out, and someone said, "That's right!" You didn't tell anyone you guessed, did you?

While playing partners, have you ever been asked a question, had a strange answer pop into your mind, and whispered it in your partner's ear? He or she looked at you like you were crazy, but blurted it out anyway? Someone stared at the question card and with a look of amazement said, *"That's right!"* What do you do? You tell everyone you told your partner the answer, right?

The game teaches a very important lesson: *The human mind really never forgets anything; however, it does not volunteer information, either.*

The only definition your mind has for "truth" is what you tell it. It gives, responds, and defines according to what you request, or what you want.

It is from those "wants" you define reality. "Reality" is your painting of what is happening. Reality will vary from person to person. *Your* definition of reality is based on *your* feelings, *your* desires, and *your* wants.

You create your own realities. It is not the situation, not the event, but what you feel that creates your sense of reality. This, in turn, gives you your understandings of what's happening in your life.

Reality 2:
You Are An Integrated System

This is very important in forming a system to control the stress in your life. For years, it was taught that a human was three separate entities — mind, body, and emotion. Each was important, but was not related to the other. Then, one day someone discovered that the three really were related. They realized the mind, the body, and the emotion work together as a system of checks and balances. Have you ever had a day when you were so mentally exhausted that you were physically tired? Have you ever had a time when you were so physically drained that mentally you had a headache? What about a time when you were so emotionally shot that you were physically a wreck?

Here is something to think about: *Your body is smarter than you are.* It responds better in working to control stress than your whole person does. On those days when the mental part of you is at load capacity, the other two provide the relief you need. Any time one of the three is about to short-circuit, the other two provide a release valve. The real danger arises when you are mentally exhausted, emotionally shot, and physically drained all at the same time. At that point there is no release valve, and the system will break down.

For checks and balances, you must learn to listen to your system. Your mind, body, and emotions warn you in plenty of time to control the impending pressure. You are an integrated system. You are designed to handle pressure as long as you are in control. At the point where pressure controls you, none of the systems are of any value. The result is a break down.

Reality 3:
You Prove Your Beliefs To Yourself

Realities 3, 4, and 5 work together as a trio of thought. You need to look at them individually, but keep in mind that each has a bearing on the others.

Everyday people tell you everything you need to know about them, and they don't even have to open their mouths to do it. If you want to know what people think or feel about a situation, watch their actions. What people believe about a situation controls their responses, and they will work to prove what they feel.

I'm sure you have been around people who worked hard to prove their beliefs. For instance, people who feel they cannot do a certain task work hard to prove to everyone they cannot do it. Encouragement from others around them may cause them to put forth a little effort, but they will make sure it is not enough to accomplish the task. When they have tried and did not achieve, they will respond with, "I told you so!"

It is amazing to watch people work to prove what they can and cannot do. When they are committed to proving they "cannot," they are defeated before they ever start. It is important you understand that *negative* is not a concept, but an action that is expressed through how you deal with a situation. There can be no question that this process creates stress. When you are working to prove a belief, there is inherent pressure to make sure you are right. This is another part of the theory of justification. What you believe, you will work to justify through your actions. You work to prove your beliefs to yourself.

Reality 4:
Behavior Follows Beliefs

It's easy to see how this answer relates to #3, **You Prove Your Beliefs to Yourself.** When you are working to prove what you feel, your behavior will be arranged to coincide with your belief. Let me take you back a few years in my life to draw an illustration.

I come from a family where I was the only male child on either side. All my parents' brothers and sisters had female children. In my home, the only males were my dad and I. Even the animals were female! Being one of a kind with three sisters made for some very interesting childhood experiences. To this day, I still say that my sisters did not like me. It is a wonder I am alive today.

I'll never forget the day my sisters decided it was time for me to learn to swim. I was five years old, and they were nine, seven, and four. At the time we lived in New Orleans, a block from a canal and five blocks from the Mississippi River. There was a playground area on the bank of the canal where the neighborhood group would always gather. This particular morning the game was not an exciting one for me. It was called "Teach Richard to Swim." I didn't want to play this game, but that did not matter to my sisters. They made the rules. They cornered me, grabbed me, picked me up and tossed me into the canal. They stood on the bank with lots of soil under their feet screaming, "Swim, Dummy! Swim!" I was in the canal with no soil under my feet, going up and down like a cork, screaming, "Help me! Help me!" A little man, who had come to the canal to enjoy fishing, heard my plea for help. After inspecting the situation, he decided that I was not going to swim, so he jumped in and pulled me to the shore.

That experience led me to believe that if I ever got into water I would drown. Any time I was around a lake, a river, a stream, or any body of water, I was terrified. My beliefs conditioned my behavior.

Have you ever had an experience that conditioned your behavior? When you feel strongly about something, it will condition your behavioral patterns.

Behavior follows beliefs. We must take this one step further and look at what happens when you try to fix it: if you try to change your behavior without examining your beliefs, no change will occur. Change that does not deal with beliefs only creates frustration. The more you understand why you do what you do, the easier it becomes to handle the frustration. Behind each action is a belief. Too many times you become so caught up in the action that you forget to deal with your feelings and beliefs. If you do not deal with your feelings, the end result will be resistance, fear, and frustration.

Reality 5:
Thoughts Create Feelings

This is the last in the trio of related answers about your beliefs and feelings. We're now getting a little deeper inside the human response system. This answer deals with a very important aspect of control. Have you ever tried to change your attitude and thought you had changed it, but then found yourself back in the same frame of mind?

Thoughts create feelings. Attitudes are not feelings; they are the expression of inner thoughts. Attitudes are not problems; they are visual symptoms of deeper issues. Attitudes are the visual projection of thoughts. By the time someone actually sees your attitude, you have already designed your feelings. You will not be able to change your attitudes until you reconstruct your thoughts about the event. Until you redefine your thoughts, your attitude will remain the same. Your attitude may change for a brief time, but your thoughts will always resurface.

There is a "cousin" term that needs a moment of attention. It's called *habit*. Have you ever seen people try to change a habit, only to end up frustrated? Most explanations of *habits* leave out a very important point. Habits are not just actions people do over and over again. Habits are actions that people do with consistency because they *get satisfaction* from them. As long as the satisfaction is there, the habits will remain. When the habits no longer provide satisfaction, people will change them by finding something that does offer the feeling of satisfaction.

Think about this: have you ever seen people who say they want to lose weight, yet no matter how hard they try, they do not succeed? What's the problem? The reason they are unsuccessful is because the habit of eating is still more satisfying than the advantages of losing weight. The same can be said about people who are always talking about their desire to stop smoking. The habit is still more satisfying than any of the alternatives.

Thoughts create feelings. Until you learn to deal with your thoughts in an open and honest way, your feelings will remain unchanged. If those feelings are a source of frustration, the longer they remain unchanged, the stronger the frustration will become.

Reality 6:
No One Can Change Another Person

For ages, this has been one of the most common creators of stress ever. Time and time again people enter jobs and relationships with the attitude that they can change another person. What we all need to know is that people are not change-oriented. People live their lives in an attempt to establish comfortable routines, not to change. Change is one of the most frightening things you can ask anyone to do. People spend their lives running *from* change, not toward it.

When I was on the counseling staff of First Baptist Church of West Palm Beach, Florida, I did a lot of premarital counseling. I enjoyed talking with young couples who were planning to spend the rest of their lives together. I would always talk to them together and then would ask the groom-to-be to go for a walk. I wanted to talk to the future bride alone. I always got strange looks from the groom, but I would assure him that it was going to be okay. After he left, I would open my desk and take out a note pad on which I had written, "Things I Plan to Change About Him After We Are Married." On the sheet were six blanks. I would ask the young lady to list the six things she intended to change about him after they were married. Most of the brides listed at least seven things! I later realized that I should have asked the grooms to make a list because they, too, have expectations of making changes.

Do you know the frustration that arises when people enter

situations intent on being creators of change? Human beings do not like change. When people enter situations bent on being creators of change, they are not met by willing participants. Most people do want to improve, *but* they don't want to have to change to get the improvement.

I'll never forget one woman who came to me totally despondent. Jane married a gentleman, knowing that he possessed traits she could not stand, but feeling confident that she could change him. She sat in my office defeated. She had given up.

She said, *"I've tried . . .I've tried every way I know to change him, but he won't change."* She paused for a few moments as if she were reliving every aspect of the relationship where she had tried to change him. Then with a look of total disgust, she said *"Do you know what? I don't think he wants to change."*

Jane had defined the lesson, even if she hadn't accepted it. No one can change another person. Trying to change another person creates an arena of personal frustration. You cannot do anything to people without their permission and cooperation. You cannot change other people. To think you can is to place yourself in a very stressful situation. Now, don't read my message incorrectly. I am not saying that people cannot change. People can change, but they—not you, must institute the change! You cannot change another person!

Reality 7:
Intuition (what you feel) Is Just As Important As Cognition (what you know)

Have you ever been in an internal tug-of-war where your

feelings were in conflict with your mind? Your mind told you to do one thing, while your gut-level feelings told you to do another. Your intuition, (what you feel about an event,) is just as important as your cognition, (what you know about the event). Sometimes what you know becomes your justified thoughts. These gut feelings are based upon feelings defined by information you have accepted as factual. Nothing is wrong with this. There is a place and time for this type of decision-making, however you must be sure this does not become your only way of understanding or defining a situation. Your thoughts can mislead you. Sometimes what you feel provides a more honest evaluation of the situation.

Don't ever just disregard your gut-level feelings. They are the most honest emotions you have. Give them their proper place among your emotions, and they will help take some of the pressure out of the decision-making process. Deny them their place and they will leave you with questions that will become nagging memories.

Reality 8:
People Talk To Hear Themselves Talk

I have seen many living illustrations of this in my lifetime, but there is one that stands above the rest. I had endured a long day of speaking on the west coast and was looking forward to leaning back and relaxing as I boarded the plane to fly home to the east coast. I took my seat, settled in, and then I saw him coming. You could tell by the way he was walking he had experienced one of those days you do not want to experience. I whispered a little prayer *"God, don't put him next to me."* It was too late. He didn't sit in the seat: he fell into the seat. I tried very hard not to notice him. I knew if I did, I would not be able to get rid of him for the entire flight.

Once he got his body and mind arranged, he was ready. He needed someone to "vent" to, not have a conversation with. He began by asking me what I did, and I knew that when I told him, the rest of the trip would be spent indulging his emotional needs. I told him I was a professional speaker and naturally he wanted to know what was my area of expertise. When I told him that my background was in psychology, his eyes grew big and he got the biggest grin on his face. He looked at me and said, *"I knew you weren't here by accident!"*

For the next four hours, I listened to his life history from two months before conception until the present. In all that time I don't think I said over ten words. If I started to say something, he would give me one of his looks that said, "Hold on. I'm not finished yet." When we arrived at the gate, he was the first one out of his seat. He grabbed my hand and said, *"Thank you! Thank you! No one has ever helped me as much as you did. Thanks for talking to me."*

I thought to myself, "I didn't talk to you. You did all the talking." Then it hit me: I had met another person who was talking to hear himself talk.

You must learn certain things about people. There are people who talk to you because they want you to talk back to them, and there are people who talk to you but do not want you to talk back to them. They need ears, not a responding mouth. If you try to talk to them, they become offended. They will even accuse you of not wanting to listen. They are not looking for answers, advice, or any form of words. What they want is someone to sit there and be their personal sounding board. They are simply talking to hear themselves.

41

Pressure exists on both sides of this fence. If you have ever been around these people, you know how much pressure they can put on you. They can stress you out in a very short while. It takes a lot of mental energy to just sit and listen. When you can respond with words, it creates a form of release. When you have to just sit there and listen, knowing they don't want you to respond, that creates pressure.

Pressure also exists for those people who want to do all the talking. What they are doing is using other people. They don't always understand what they are doing. They don't see themselves as using others; they just know they need someone who will listen. Eventually, other people will become less willing to lend them an ear. The harder it becomes for them to find a set of ears without a mouth, the more rejected they feel.

People talk to hear themselves talk. The more you understand this, the easier it will become for you to understand why communication is such a huge challenge and the quicker you will be able to recognize this type of personality. When you can recognize these people, you can control the pressure they place on you. Part of controlling pressure is recognizing what creates it!

Reality 9:
Each One Of Us Is Alone

This may be the hardest of all the answers for you to understand. I know each time I talk about this during a program, I get a lot of strange looks from people. "Each one of us is alone" is a hard statement to accept. Most people don't like the feeling of being alone. We live our lives desiring and seeking the approval of others, sometimes at the cost of our personal happiness.

People who spend their lives seeking the approval of others create a lot of stress for themselves. They spend their lives being what others want them to be, rather than becoming what they really can become. These people have not learned the difference between being "lonely" and being "alone." You need to understand this if you want to control the stress in your life.

"Lonely" is when you find yourself alone with you and don't like it. Being by yourself is one of the most frightening things that can happen to you. You do not enjoy your own company and always want to be with someone else because you know when you are alone you must deal with all the things you are running from in your life.

"Alone" is when you find yourself alone with you and love it. You don't need people to be happy, because you realize that other people do not create happiness. *Happiness comes from within you.* You don't need people to feel secure, because you realize that if people can give you security, they can also take it away. You don't need people in order to feel worthwhile. You realize that what other people offer you is their definition of you based on what *they* want you to be. If you accept that, then you become *their* creation and not who you really are.

When you understand this concept, then you can also understand the difference between "need" and "want." If you need people, you live with blinders that hinder your vision. "Need" limits your ability to see and know the value of people and events. If your understanding is based on need that is all you will see. As long as the situation or person meets your needs, things are great. If it does not meet your needs, then what do you do? You become critical. Most of your criticisms are based upon the fact something has not gone the way you needed it to go, or someone has not done what you expected them to do.

"Want" is a different story. When want is stronger than need, you see through a more mature set of eyes. *Want removes restrictions.* Want accepts as is; need demands change. Want creates an attitude of freedom; need constructs a personal prison cell. Want makes one responsible for self; need tries to make others responsible for what has or has not been.

In this world, you must understand you are alone. You are responsible for yourself. Others may share your world, but they are not your world. They may fill your world, but they are only there because at this moment they share a point of common existence. What you do with your sphere of life must be your decision, not one made for you by someone else. Otherwise, you lose your uniqueness and become just another clone in a world of copies.

Each one of us is alone. The more secure you become in that thought, the more freedom you will grant the others in your life. The more comfortable you become with your "aloneness," the more willing you will be to grant others the space they need to be themselves. People who smother or place restrictions on the others in their lives do so out of their own insecurities. The more secure you are in your aloneness, the less threatened you are by others.

Aloneness allows people to stop focusing on differences and start looking for how they connect. Instead of being threatened by the difference, you can champion the right to be alone and unique. Instead of working to make other people be like you or make them into what you need them to become, you can begin to discover the uniqueness of the relationship. Instead of being disappointed by the fact others don't meet your expectations, you can treasure their personal touches to your life and search for the gifts they offer you. Only when you free others of your needs, can you discover who they really are and what they really mean to your life. That is a great stress control!

Reality 10:
Change Is Inevitable

This is mandatory for stress control. I believe change is one of the top creators of stress. People live their lives in an attempt to establish comfortable routines, not to change. We will explore this idea in depth as we walk through your Stress House and its four rooms. *Most people feel they would be a lot happier if they did not have to deal with change.* Change is viewed as a stressful, negative thing in life.

You must understand that change is inevitable. The stress is created in the resistance, not in the fact of change. There is growth in change. Without change there is no growth — reality is, things die. You need to see change as a natural part of life's order. The more you understand that everything will change, whether you want it or not, the easier the process becomes.

Change is only an enemy when it is defined as a threat. When change is understood (not necessarily agreed to, but understood), it can be seen as a friend. Change is inevitable. One of the secrets to stress control is working to understand what the change means, rather than working to keep it from happening.

Reality 11:
The More You Resist, The More It Persists

I really don't think this answer needs a lot of defining. You have experienced it many times. Things don't just go away. They must be dealt with. Not only do things not disappear, they often get worse. The more you resist, the more it persists. Situations demand action. That demand might create stress, but stress also comes with postponement. Postponement creates a lingering stress that just keeps gnawing at you. That stress grows each time you resist. The longer anything persists, the more energy it requires. The more energy it requires, the greater the pressure that is created. Dealing with the event, rather than postponing the inevitable is a great stress control.

Reality 12:
You Already Know What To Do

You already know what to do with 99% of the things you struggle with in your life. You create stress by justifying not doing what you *know* needs to be done. One of the greatest stress controls is to practice acceptance, rather than denial. Denial is our way of running from necessary action. Acceptance is the mature pattern of growth. You already know what you need to do — *so do it!*

Dennis' email reply to me was simply, *"I knew you were going to say that."*

My response was, "How did you know how I was going to respond?"

"Richard, I knew the answer to the question when I wrote it. I just didn't want to hear me say it, so I looked for you to tell me what I already knew."

Life is not about not knowing; life is about doing what you know you should do. I believe that many people who have come to me over the years for counseling have not come looking for answers, but to have me tell them what they already knew, but didn't want to hear themselves say. You already know what to do!

REVIEW OF
ANSWERS

DIRECTIONS: Read each answer and circle your response concerning that answer.

1. We create our own realities. Agree Disagree

2. The human system is
   an integrated system. Agree Disagree

3. People prove their beliefs
   to themselves. Agree Disagree

4. Behavior follows beliefs. Agree Disagree

5. Thoughts create feelings. Agree Disagree

6. No one can change
   another person. Agree Disagree

7. People talk to hear
   themselves. Agree Disagree

8. Each one of us is alone. Agree Disagree

9. Intuition is just as important
   as cognition. Agree Disagree

10. Change is inevitable. Agree Disagree

11. The more you resist,
    the more it persists. Agree Disagree

12. You already know. Agree Disagree

CHAPTER 5
The Business Room

We will tour your Stress House room by room, look at who occupies each of the rooms with you, who *should* occupy each room with you, and *what* things you need to change in each room to make your Stress House manageable for your life.

The largest room in your four-room house is the business room. You may find yourself spending more time in this room than any of the other rooms.

Most occupants view the business room as the number one room for stress. Most occupants also view it as the most important room in the house. This is easy to understand when you realize the control this room has over the other three rooms. The business room generally defines your lifestyle. It creates the financial security that is used to decorate the other rooms. If the business room lacks stability, it will have an effect on the stability of the other rooms. If the stability in this room changes, it causes pressure and may even cause upheaval in the other rooms.

Remember that people live their lives to be comfortable, not to change. Anytime change comes to any room of the house, it becomes an unwelcome guest. Change is an intruder to a comfortable routine. Change is an interior designer that sometimes decorates without the owner's permission.

Change comes to the business room in a couple of forms. The first is a promotion or an increase in business profits. This can mean an increase in income. It can also redesign your life.

An increase in income is exciting! The occupant begins to think of things the money will allow to be done in the

49

other rooms. It's fantastic when dreams can become reality because of the financial strength of the business room; yet, the increase of money can also create pressure. Isn't it amazing how an increase in income creates an increase in expenditures! With growth in your dreams comes an increase in the cost of fulfilling them. Many times an increase in income does not alleviate existing pressure, it just redefines it.

With a promotion also comes a change in your routine. Routines are comfortable because they create sameness. Routines are filled with definable patterns. Definable patterns are easy because they contain very few surprises.

Have you ever seen a person work for a promotion? It is his drive; it is his dream. Then, it becomes reality and the reality creates pressure. It means redirection and re-orientation. The reality means that what was can no longer be.

Not long ago I was doing an in-house program for a company in Cleveland. At the end of my program, Steve wanted to know if I had time to talk with him. He was bright, ambitious and driven by a strong desire to succeed. He had been with the company for five years. He started as a young, inexperienced salesperson, and in a year-and-a-half, he had become the number one salesperson. This created a lot of pressure on him from the other salespeople in the company. He was not only the youngest in seniority, but also in age. He was ten years younger than any of the others. Because of his sales record, he had received a lot of recognition and commendation from the company. One day the vice president of marketing approached him about becoming sales manager. Wow! That's what he wanted. That was his dream. His answer was an immediate "yes."

He had served as a general sales manager for one year

when he came to me. I'll never forget his opening words. "This job as sales manager is real hell."

I could tell by the look in his eyes the stress of the situation was eating him alive. He had to do something to control the situation or it would destroy him.

With a great amount of intensity he continued his words. "I thought this was what I wanted. I came to this company with a desire to succeed and the dream of being general sales manager. Now, I have the position, and I would give anything to just be back in sales."

He paused briefly, as though reflecting on what he had just said. After a couple of minutes he continued. "I came to this position with a lot of dreams and changes I knew could improve the company. Do you know what my ideas got me? Criticism. Many people in the sales force resented the fact that I had been given the position. They felt that because they had been there longer than I that they deserved the promotion. Now, any suggestions I make, they resist. I don't want to use the position as one of power, but they are leaving me no option. If I am going to do what I set out to do, I have to go to war with them, and that is not my style."

I stopped him and asked if he had tried using upper management as a bridge. He looked at me with daggers in his eyes, and I knew before he answered that I had asked the wrong question.

"That's a joke," he said. "Sure I went to them. A few months ago I admitted to myself that I didn't know what to do, and believe me that was tough. I have always handled everything alone. I have always felt that asking for help was a sign of weakness, but I was at my wits end. I was out of ideas. I went to the vice president of marketing, and boy was

51

that a mistake! He made me feel like an idiot. Rather than listening to me, the minute I started telling him my problem he interrupted and started criticizing me. Let me tell you, I blew my stack. I reminded him that when I agreed to take the position, he promised to always be there to help me. He didn't mean it. It was just a way of buttering me up. Then, do you know what he had the audacity to say? He told me if the fire was too hot in the kitchen, I could always get out. Can you believe that?"

Now, the look that had been pain was one of anger. "I could get out. I didn't ask to be there in the first place."

He paused and then said, "Well, that's not really true. I thought it was what I wanted. Sure, I could get out, but where would I go? I can't go back to sales. I don't want to stay in this position. I guess I have one other choice—that's to leave the company. I don't want to do that, but what else can I do?"

What had happened to Steve? The promotion had taken him out of his comfortable routine. The change had demanded a redirection, a re-orientation, and an exchange of philosophies. In the beginning that was okay, but the new routine was not comfortable. It was not what he wanted, and Steve had to learn a very painful and stressful lesson.

Once a routine has been changed, you cannot go back to it.

Once the business room, or any room, has been redecorated, you cannot go back into it and recreate what was. Doing that will simply create more pressure. Trying to go back to what was is never the answer. It may seem like a solution, but it only creates more pressure and a greater struggle.

A promotion can also cause a change in location. Moving your residence is always stressful, no matter how many people are involved.

Moving means taking everyone in the family out of their routines. Can you feel the pressure the business room would exert on the family room? The other occupants who share the house might understand, but that does not mean they will accept it very well.

What if the spouse has a career? What if the children have established roles of importance?

Let's say a divorce has already rearranged the house, but there was still a sharing of time and people in the family and social rooms. The promotion would mean a move that would make it impossible for that form of sharing to continue. Can you sense the pain, the struggle, the stress this could create for everyone?

Career couples in Corporate America often must deal with the stress of relocation. Jeff and Susie are perfect examples of this. Jeff was bright, creative, and climbing the corporate ladder. Susie, his wife, also had a highly successful career. Jeff's company approached him with an offer that was more than he could have hoped for, but the promotion would have meant moving from Los Angeles to New York City.

Susie and Jeff spent hours talking about it. If Jeff didn't take the position, his career with this company would be over. Oh, he could stay, but he would be placed on the back shelf. There he would be lost for eternity.

On the other hand, Susie's career had just taken off. Two years prior she had opened her own shop. It had been a real struggle, as well as a financial drain for them. Just recently, things had turned around. Business was booming, and her investment in time, energy and emotions was paying off. She couldn't take it with her.

They talked about two households, but the distance would make that impossible. Besides, the new position would demand a lot of Jeff's time.

You can imagine they had a lot of stressful moments. Finally, they decided that with all things considered, the move would be wrong. Jeff was put on a shelf. Being the creative person he was, he could not handle that. He soon left the company and went to work for what had been the competition. Today he is doing well in management, and Susie's business has blossomed into four stores.

Recently, Jeff told me that his former employer offered him the position that created the original struggle, only this time he would not have to move. Jeff did not accept the offer. He knew you could not go back with effectiveness into a room that had already been redecorated.

Within the business room you can also experience demotions as well as promotions. The financial strength of the business room is what defines the budget and spending habits of the family and social rooms. These rooms are given their stability by the money generated in the business room. People grow accustomed to a certain level of income. If that income is increased, the re-orientation is fun. If the change is a decrease, the result is pressure. It is very difficult to rearrange financial philosophies when a habit of spending has been established.

A salary rollback also means the family room must readjust. This creates pressure for the occupants, who have become accustomed to a certain level of living.

I was visiting Ron, a psychologist friend, who has a practice in New Orleans. The conversation dealt with the effect that the energy crisis was having on people's upperscale lifestyle. Now, the money is not there. They cannot afford to drive the Mercedes, to dine out each and every meal, to throw the posh parties they once did. Now, their lifestyles need to be readjusted. Reality does not always create actuality.

My friend Ron said that many of these people, who *cannot*, are living in a world where they are pretending that they still *can*. Some have undergone severe mental and emotional trauma—even to the point of committing suicide.

Ron also said that this dramatic financial adjustment has created severe tension in the family room. Many of the spouses, who have become accustomed to the freedom of spending, now encounter the unfamiliar pressure that comes from financial instability. This, in turn, has created an arena of blame. One blames the other for the forced changes. Then, the blame is placed on the spender for not being more thrifty with the money that was earned.

What they are simply doing is dumping their stress on each other. Rather than working together for a plan of readjustment, they are spending their frustrated energy hurting each other. This can take a relationship that has been secure and turn it into a crisis center.

There are several other creators of stress in the business room that demand attention. Again, it is important for you to realize that the pressure in this room will find its way into other rooms of your Stress House. The more you are able to control the pressure in this room, the easier it will be to control the stress in the other rooms.

*People who work to eliminate
stress become stressful.
People who learn to control
stress become creative.*

Stress in the business room is more mental than
emotional. Both factors are present in each room, but you will
find that one tends to dominate. The dominant factor (mental
or emotional) will vary with the room.

The Stressors

Let's look at a few of the other creators of stress, or
stressors, in the business room. These are, by no means, all of
them, but are the ones I have found to be the most visible.

The first stressor: *uncontrollable events.* Many times you
have no control over what occurs in this room. The pressure
here is in knowing what is happening and not being able to do
anything about it. This is especially tough if you are a creative
person who is always looking for a way to accomplish things.
When your hands are tied because of something you have no
control over, the end result is pressure and frustration.

Nothing is a greater example of this than the downsizing
that Corporate America is going through today. Thousands of
people have been given their pink slips, and there is nothing
they can do about it. It is out of their control.

The result is a feeling of betrayal. Many people have
invested years of their lives only to be tossed aside by those at
the top who have made profitability more important than the
loyalty of the people who generated the possibility of making
money. You think that hasn't added stress to people? But

again, it is out of their control.

Our second stressor: *unpredictable events.* Many times, unpredictable events are more stressful than uncontrollable events. That's because these are sneak attacks. You know there are uncontrollable events. You may even know they are coming and can plan for them. With unpredictable events you are not aware they are going to happen. Then whamo! They hit you and take all your mental energy.

Anytime you are hit with what you were not prepared for, the end result will be frustration and pressure. Anytime you are forced to deal with what you did not anticipate, you will use three to four times the normal mental energy to deal with the situation. Unpredictable events make you shift mental gears. Here you are mentally going in one direction and without warning, the unpredictable happens. Now, in the middle of one thought pattern, you must shift gears. Not only is that tough, but it also means pressure.

Walter came to me with tears in his eyes. I had spent the morning speaking about "Embracing Change." I knew he was hurting. I knew he needed to talk but was embarrassed by his emotional presence.

I walked over, looked him in the eyes and said in a gentle way, "Would you like to take a walk with me?"

He didn't say a word; he just nodded and I motioned for us to walk. It didn't take long for him to start his emotional unloading.

"I didn't enjoy what you talked about tonight. Yet, I know what you were talking about was what I needed. Richard, I have worked for this company for twenty-five years. I knew the new ownership was looking to make some changes. I even approached the owner and we talked about my role in the new environment. He looked me straight in the eye and told me I didn't have anything to worry about. They knew how valuable I was, and they wanted me to help in the transition."

He paused and he worked to control the anger that was filling his being.

"It wasn't a week later that I was handed my walking papers. I would have never predicted that. Not after what I had been told. I tried to see the owner, but he wouldn't see me. How could they do that to me? How could they just throw me away like a piece of stale bread? I was there for them, but I guess that didn't matter. All they saw was they could replace me with someone they could pay less. Guess I know what my commitment meant!"

Walter was experiencing a major blow that affected every part of his life. He really didn't see it coming, since he had talked with his new boss about what was happening. Knowing that he was going to be able to "embrace the change" his life was experiencing was somewhat of a relief. The pressure in his business room was going to affect every other room in his house.

The third stressor: *too much or not enough business activity.* Have you noticed in the business world there is no middle ground? It is either feast or famine. It is all hog or no sausage. Either extreme creates pressure.

What happens when there is not enough business? What is the pressure? The pressure is *money*. It takes money to operate a business. When there is no business activity and cash flow is not there, the pressure is felt from the top of the organization to the bottom.

I am amazed how companies fail to plan for the slow times. Every company has them. Any company that has been in business for two years should be able to determine the slack income times. You plan and prepare for these. Then when they happen, they will not drain company reserves.

When there is too much business activity, there is also pressure. This pressure is *time*. When business activity is slow, you sit around wishing it were busy. When it gets busy, you find yourself wishing things would slow down.

Have you ever come to the realization you are no longer president of your life, but you have been demoted to maintenance supervisor? How many times have you started your day with ten things on your "To Do" list, only to finish your day with twenty items still remaining? Time that controls you is pressure. Demands on your time that are not met will create pressure. The more things there are for you to do, the more pressure you create for yourself to do them.

Too much or not enough business activity is pressure. It is a never-ending circle with no visible exit.

The next creator of stress in the business room is *the people you work with each day.* This has become an increasing creator of stress.

If you are in a management position, the stress comes in trying to get people to be productive. One reason this pressure exists is the misguided philosophy of management. For years we were all taught that it was management's job to motivate people. That one philosophical point is probably responsible for about forty percent of the pressure that managers experience.

Here is reality: you cannot motivate anyone. To believe you can is to set yourself up for disappointment, frustration and pressure.

You cannot motivate anyone, just like you cannot change

anyone. The sooner management realizes and admits that fact, the sooner some of the pressure will be relieved. If you *could* motivate someone, here is what reality would be: *the motivation will only last as long as you are around.* How many times have you seen this happen? A manager creates motivation, goes to do another task, and returns only to have to create the motivation all over again.

Motivation is an individual responsibility. All management can do is create an environment driven by positive energy. The individual must create his or her own dream. The basis for real motivation is a dream. Without a dream, which is an anticipated reality, there will be no motivation.

I really believe one of the most stressful positions a human can hold is management. Why? Because most people are more interested in surviving than they are in growing.

There is also pressure if you are an employee of a company. Have you noticed that the majority of the work done is accomplished by the minority? Most people who go to a job each day do not go to *work*, but to watch. These watchers create stress for the others in the organization. They do not carry their share of the load and this makes it difficult for others. I have always been amazed at how a worker will try to cover-up for a watcher. He will punish himself harder. All this does is create frustration, pressure, and validate the lack of action of the one being protected.

Our fifth stressor: *the inability to manage your time effectively.* Have you ever gone to a seminar on time management, returned, and had your schedule get all messed up because of the time you spent at the time management seminar? Time management is not the problem, but a symptom of the real illnesses. Time management is only pressure when

60

you do not understand what causes that pressure. I have learned through the years of counseling on a personal level and coaching in the business arena, that there are three causes of time *mis*management: lack of organization, lack of setting realistic priorities and failure to listen.

Anytime you are not organized, you will struggle with time management. Do you really know what organization is? *Organization is a plan that accomplishes a task before it becomes a crisis.* When you postpone something until it becomes "a must," it takes a different type of mental energy to get the job done. That mental energy is not creative energy, but crisis mentality.

Now, you may be thinking to yourself, "I work better and accomplish more when the pressure is on me."

That statement is true only if you are controlling the pressure. If organization is a challenge for you, procrastination is there somewhere. You put off and put off until you can't put off any longer. Then, the task takes on a different meaning. At that point you may be *doing*, but you are not really using all your creative skills because you do not have time to think and experiment. There is only time *to do something.*

Organization is really very simple. It is controlling procrastination. It is accomplishing a task before it becomes a crisis.

Understand a lack of set priorities will cause you all kinds of time management struggles. You must learn that priority is not just a word; it is energy. How many times have you called something a priority, but never given it the proper energy? Your result — it didn't get done.

The things you give energy to are what you consider your real priorities.

Another cause of time mismanagement is the failure to listen. Many of us are poor listeners because we have never been taught listening skills. Have you ever been in a conversation, met someone new, been introduced, and within five minutes not be able to remember their name? Have you ever found yourself formulating what you are going to say when the person who is talking stops, and because of that you don't hear what they are saying?

Listening is not a skill you are born with. It is a skill you have to develop. Listening takes patience. Listening takes a commitment to hear. Listening begins when you feel the other person is valuable enough that you can learn from his or her words and actions. Listening is hearing with your ears *and* your eyes.

People who do not listen will struggle with time management. They will find the task requiring more time and energy because they did not listen. They will ask questions that have already been answered.

Time-management is not
the illness;
it is the symptom.

The pressure is not from a lack of time, but from a lack of control. To control the time takes organization, disciplined priorities, and the ability to listen.

Another stressor in our business room: *expectations.* Expectations are simply desires you would like to fulfill. The pressure comes when the desires are there, energy is expended, and the desires are still unfulfilled.

There are three participants in your life that create

expectations for your life: business, family and personal. If you are an employee, the company you work for has expectations of you. These expectations can create real pressure when they are not met. Anything that is given to you without your agreement will not have your total commitment. This will result in frustration and pressure.

There are also expectations placed on you by your family. All families have expectations for the occupant of the business room. Remember what we talked about earlier: the financial stability of the business room creates the possibilities for the family room. If the financial stability is not there, the expectations of the family room will not be met. The end result will be frustration and pressure.

There are also personal expectations: you have dreams you want for yourself. Inside of you are things you constantly dream about having, doing, or experiencing. Many times these are driving forces in your life. When you realize they cannot be achieved the result is frustration and stress.

Expectations are a source of strength; expectations can define direction and desire. But expectations can also create mental and emotional letdown. Just remember that stress can result from either side of expectations.

Another stressor in our business room is an animal all to itself: *the media.* I have come to believe that, next to change, this is the second largest creator of stress you deal with in this room. Have you ever been part of an event covered by the media, read about it in the paper and wondered where you were? Have you ever read or heard something concerning your company or client that was reported by the media before you ever got wind of it? I learned a long time ago that the purpose of the media is not to report news, but to create sensationalism.

63

The media does <u>not</u> always report the news; it reports events in such a way that they *sell*. Much of what is done in the name of "journalistic privilege" is really done in the name of "profit without ethics."

So many people believe that anything the media reports is absolute truth. The power and responsibility of the media is constantly being abused by itself. When the media is above being judged right or wrong, it is dangerous. When it does not have to be responsible, it sets itself up as judge and jury. In this position it continually creates pressure on you, the public eye and ear.

The last of our stressors in the business room is *ambition*. Ambition can be the spark that lights your fire, or the fuse that makes you explode.

Has your drive to do something ever gotten out of control? Has your ambition ever consumed your thoughts and time? When that happens, you are no longer in control. Your ambition has become your compulsion. Ambition is healthy as long as it is kept in check. When it controls you, it becomes a creator of stress.

You must constantly keep your dreams in front of you. You must constantly remind yourself of the value of other people. You must remain in control of your dreams, rather than being driven by only ambition. When ambition controls you, you will lose sight of reality. When ambition controls you, you will do anything to make things happen. The amount of stress it will place on you is amazing. Situations are no longer fun.

A man named Harry said it to me this way, "I don't care who I have to walk over, bull my way through or hurt. I am going to win!"

I thought he was kidding, but after being around him for a

brief time, I knew this was who he really was. The challenge is that there are a number of Harry's out there. There are several whose ambition controls them and makes them dangerous and stressful.

Business Room In Review

The business room is the largest room in your house. Its pressures are great. It is important for you to remember this room creates financial freedom for the other rooms. This room defines possibilities.

To exercise control in this room, you must understand each source of stress. We just talked about the most visible stressors, but in your daily life you can probably list more. You cannot begin to define controls until you can be honest about the things that are creators of stress in your business room.

Once the stressors are defined, you can determine your options. Options themselves will bring a certain amount of relief. When a situation controls you, you lose your ability to be objective. When your objectivity is gone, not only are you blinded to reality, but you are also caught in a maze that destroys your direction. Without a defined direction you are a stress-filled nightmare.

Never forget that there is always more than one option (possibility) in *any* situation. When you can see possibilities, you can control the stress. When you lose sight of your options, the stress of the situation controls you.

CHAPTER 6
The Family Room

The next room we will tour in your four-room house is the family room. The square footage in this room is only a few feet less than that of the business room. In most peoples' lives the family room is constantly in conflict with the business room.

Most people think that the family room is next in line when it comes to pressure. It is important for you to understand that the pressure in this room is more emotional than mental. You will notice that this is the opposite of the business room, which was more mental than emotional.

The interactions in the business room mostly involve people with whom you *do not* have emotional ties. The ties are mostly mental. In the family room, you find yourself dealing with situations and people with whom you *do* have emotional ties. This changes the type of pressure created in this room. When you are dealing with people with whom you do not have emotional ties, you treat the situation with a different level of energy. Mental pressure is real, although the energy drain is different from that which is created by emotional pressure.

People with whom you share emotional ties affect you at a different level. The energy they take carries a personal intensity. That personal intensity can create a pressure that is all consuming.

Roy is a good example of the difference the emotional ties make. He is in management at a large electronics company. His secretary has been with him for five years, and recently her son and Roy's daughter were in the same hospital at the same time and both were having a tonsillectomy. Roy

67

said he was concerned about her son, but was a nervous wreck about his daughter. The difference was the strong emotional ties he had to his own daughter although he cared about her son.

Stress in your family room will create a different type of pressure. Many times that emotional drain will seem heavy and very hard to deal with, especially in a positive way. It can leave you exhausted and sometimes ill.

There are several creators of pressure in the family room, but I'm only going to address the four largest creators of family pressure that I have dealt with in my experience of counseling and coaching for the past 25 years.

It is important to remember the relationships the rooms have with each other. Pressure in any one room can be found in another room. Something that happened in the family room may be carried to work the next day, thus affecting the business room.

You cannot bottle up pressure in any one room. It will creep out and make its presence known in other rooms. Even pressure that is dealt with in the room of its origin may have an effect on the other rooms.

The Stressors

Our first stressor in the family room is *a lack of quality family time.* It really is true that there is a vast difference between spending time and spending *quality* time together.

Once when I was doing a radio talk show, a caller said something very profound: "We are together a lot, but even when we are together, we are apart."

She described many of the relationships I have seen.

People spend time together, but the time lacks quality energy. It is very possible to be present, but absent at the same time. This is where we hear the statement, "He/she is just not there for me."

I'll never forget this one couple who came to me for counseling. Pat was in his office each morning by 7:00 a.m. and would get home at 6:00 p.m., but would work until 10:00 p.m. or 11:00 p.m. at home. When they went out, it was always business-related.

His wife's complaint was, "He never spends time with me."

This was Pat's reply: "What do you want from me? I'm home every evening by six o'clock. I don't go out running around with the guys. I know other women who would be happy to be in your place. It seems that with you, I'm damned if I do and damned if I don't. There is no pleasing you."

With hurt in her eyes, she said, "I know you're home every evening, but what do you do when you're home? All you ever do is sit at your desk and work. You don't talk to me. You don't do anything with me. You may be home physically, but mentally and emotionally you are somewhere else. I sometimes wished that if all you were going to do is work, you would stay at the office. At least then, I wouldn't have to look at you locked up in your silent corner."

Pat did not understand the difference between just being present and giving quality time. A lack of shared quality time creates pressure with those whom you are emotionally tied to.

With more and more women having their own business rooms, this has become a growing struggle. When both spouses have a demanding business room, the pressure is really felt in the family room. Home should be a refuge from the pressures of the business room. In the family room, you don't want to make major business decisions. In the family room, you don't want to have intense interaction. You want this room to be quiet and comfortable; yet you are not alone in this room. There are others who share this room with you. They are not always at the same level-of-need as you. They want you to be the person they need. When you aren't there, the result is tension and pressure.

Quality time is time that is filled with understanding. Quality time is time where each occupant is in tune with the others. Quality time does not mean you have to be doing something. It can be a silent time; it can be a time of doing; it is a time where each understands and responds to the other's presence with respect.

In the story of Pat, his wife would not have minded if he had made time for her. Instead, he made her feel like an outsider in his life. She felt she wasn't important.

Remember, we as humans are more emotional than logical. We all want to know that we matter. Whether someone matters to you or not is defined by the quality of time you give, not the quantity. When people know you are there, but sense you would rather be somewhere else, there is pressure. When people question whether or not you value them, there will be pressure.

People who are important in your life need your time. People who are emotionally tied to your life need your quality time. If quality time is not given, they will fight for it. If quality time is not there, they will create pressure.

The second stressor in the family room is financial need. You go to bed, turn the light off, snuggle up under the covers, close your eyes, and what do you hear?. . . Your checkbook crying on top of the dresser!

In the discussion on the business room, we talked about financial pressure. It's a fact that it's easier to adjust financially upward than it is to adjust financially downward. Households need money to operate. When the money is not there, the occupants find themselves under pressure. In the past couple of years, I have found financial pressure to be the second largest struggle the family room faces on a daily basis.

Twenty-five years ago if a couple wanted something, but could not afford it, what did they do? They saved for it. Today, that is not the case. A couple gets married and then they purchase everything they want . . . on credit! Research has not really shown the impact that plastic money has had on the family room. It is easy to say, "Charge it." Then, the bills come. Sure, you can pay them off over time, but each month the money has to go out. It is so easy these days to become financially strapped.

Being financially strapped makes it hard or sometimes impossible to do other things you've wanted to do. It's amazing the arguments that are created when you want to do something and your mate informs you the money is not there. This easily becomes a real source of conflict and pressure.

Too many households operate on the philosophy of uncontrolled spending. There is no discipline when it comes to money. A lack of discipline and a policy of non-budgetary, uncontrolled spending creates pressure.

Ruth loves Arthur! There is no doubt about that. They have been married twelve years and are farther behind today financially than they were twelve years ago.

Arthur lives in a world of positive affirmations that are really designed to cover up what he doesn't want to face.

Each and every time Ruth wants to talk about their financial situation, Arthur tells her not to worry. Things are going to be just great.

He will look at her and ask, "Do you believe in me?"

For a long time she played the game he kept sucking her into. She would look at him and say, "Of course I do."

Yet inside she was screaming at the top of her lungs. She wanted Arthur to slow down and face the issue that was in front of them — namely the lack of dollars to pay for their bills.

Finally, she had had it. Arthur was a personality who lived in his imagination. He was always working on his next great idea. His behavior was that he would start things, run into a wall and walk away. Each new idea had a price tag associated to it. Each new idea took money they didn't have, but would take from their credit cards. His last great idea had not only taken the rest of their savings, but also maxed out all their credit cards. This was the last straw for Ruth.

Finally, she cornered Arthur and told him, "I have had enough. You have me living in depression. You have these great ideas and they take money. In fact, they have taken all our money. Arthur, I love you and believe in you, but I can't live this way."

Again, he tried his standard procedure by telling her not to worry. This time it didn't stop her.

"You are talking about believing in what you are doing and I'm trying to figure out how to get food for us and the kids. Arthur, you live in your own world and don't stop to see what is happening here. We have nowhere to turn. We are broke and I don't see any way out. You have got to stop and help me!"

Ruth and Arthur are no different than so many families.

They push themselves to the financial edge and then stress out over how they are going to take care of everything. The pressure is huge; the tension between them grows; the family room becomes a place where the lack of dollars feeds the confusion and frustrations.

Our third stressor is *role expectations*. With the addition of the working mother, role expectations have become an increasing source of stress. For generations it was taught that there were certain chores to be done in the family room that only a woman should do. Many households lived through similar experiences like The Tuesday Shirt.

The Tuesday Shirt

It's Tuesday morning and every Tuesday morning for ten years he has worn his blue dress shirt. He gets up, has his shower, walks into the bedroom where blindfolded he can find that blue shirt. Out of the bedroom she hears a scream, and then he appears holding a naked hanger and proclaims, "Where's my blue shirt?"

Realizing what is happening, she replies in a panic-stricken tone, "What day is this?"

"Blue Shirt day."

"Oh, honey…I'm so sorry. You know I had to work late last night, and I was so tired when I got home I didn't even realize today would be Tuesday. Your blue shirt is in the laundry basket. You'll just have to wear something else."

His eyes get real big, and he responds in a tone of total selfishness: *"You know I wear my blue shirt every Tuesday. I don't understand why it isn't clean. I have to have my blue shirt!"*

73

Feeling the rage rising inside her, she responds. "What do you want me to do?"

"Wash it!"

Now *her* eyes get real big, and she screams, "Wash it yourself!"

Role expectations are pressure points. How many times have you experienced pressure because you were not performing the role expected of you? If the major occupants in the family room are going to have a business room, there must be some communication concerning the necessary functions of the family room. It must be understood that when each spouse has a business room, the family room must be a partnership. Responsibilities must be shared.

This understanding has become common with many young couples. When they marry, each brings a career to the relationship. From the beginning, they share household responsibilities.

The real challenge arises when the household is accustomed to the wife being at home and handling the household duties. One day she walks in and announces that since the children are older and in school all day, she feels it is time for her to fulfill some of her dreams. She is going back to work. The husband says, "That's good. I'm all for it. I'm behind you one hundred percent."

What he is really saying is, "I'm for it as long as it doesn't upset your functions here at home." It should be understood that when it comes to changes in role expectations, men are not as adaptable. A man who is accustomed to the woman being at home may tell her it's okay for her to work, but when she starts working and the household routine is disturbed, the end results are friction and pressure.

74

How many times have you seen pressure in the family room because dinner was late, the laundry was not done, or some chore was not done because mom was not there? Have you ever seen children place pressure on mom because they felt mom should *always* be there doing things for them?

I believe in being there for your kids, but I do not believe in living your entire life for your children. Children are masters at creating parental guilt trips. Have you ever seen a parent sacrifice a personal dream because the child does not want the parent to do it? My question has always been—who's the parent? Children can create unreal role expectations. Most of the time this evolves because parents teach their children to be dependent rather than independent.

When children grow up with their parents doing everything for them, they seldom mature with a sense of responsibility. This created dependency results in a prison for the parents. This created dependency develops an irresponsible child. In the long run, the pressure on parent and child is unhealthy and destructive. Being a parent is a responsibility, not a prison. Being a parent does not mean that you should live your life a slave to the desires of your children.

The last stressor in the family room is *home expectations*. Every home has a set of dreams it is working to accomplish. Whether it be redecorating or adding onto the house or creating some sense of newness, these home expectations are emotionally important to the stability of the home. As long as the occupants in the family room can see progress being made toward those dreams, the pressure is acceptable and controllable. If the occupants cannot see movement they consider positive, the pressure created becomes frustration and puts the room in conflict.

Home expectations are important. They create the dreams for the occupants. They also provide the family room with energy and direction. Without these expectations the family room becomes a mentally and emotionally vacant room.

What You Need In Your Family Room

The family room is the second largest room in your Stress House. It is important for you to remember that the commitment here is more emotional than mental. Again, it is important you remember that people with whom you have emotional ties require a different energy than those with whom you have mental ties.

The stress in the room must be understood and controlled. The major element of control revolves around communication. There may be a great deal of idle chatter, but if very little real communication goes on in this room the stress will be greater.

It is amazing how difficult it is to talk to those with whom you have emotional ties. You know you need to talk, but for many reasons communication does not happen until the situation becomes critical. At this point the communication is panic-driven and out of control. Words are spoken through pain and frustration, rather than through controlled understanding.

Whether we want to admit it or not, most of us are poor communicators. We would rather talk than listen. Communication demands the ability to hear and listen. Effective communication demands a controlled environment.

Effective communication requires:

1. a sender
2. a receiver
3. an understood message

Poor communication includes:

1. two senders
2. no receiver
3. a misunderstood message

The key to controlling the pressure in the family room is communication. When effective communication is present, pressure is dealt with properly and not allowed to fester and explode.

CHAPTER 7
The Social Room

The third room in your Stress House is the playroom.
This room is properly called the social room. This room
carries an important key to controlling the stress in your life.
When you use it correctly, it gives you the needed space for
relaxation.

Here's the danger about this room: rather than just
spending some time in it, some people have chosen to take up
residency in the social room of their lives.

This has made this room the number one room for escape.
When the pressure is too great in the business room, where do
most people run? They run to their social room. When the
pressure is too great in the family room, where do they go?
They go to their social room. When people run from having
to face themselves in their personal room, where do they go?
They go to their social room.

The social room has now become the room for escape.
Why this room? In this room, you can become anyone or
anything you desire. In this room, you can pretend, and
pretending is one of the most popular ways of dealing with
problems in this country.

I'll never forget meeting Brenda. I was doing a program
for her company in St. Cloud, Minnesota. She came to me
after I had spoken, wanting to know if I would talk with her.
She was a very confused and frustrated young lady.

The last few months of her life had seen her Stress
House go through major renovation. Her business room was
in a major uproar. She was in sales and statistics showed she
was good at what she did. She was not number one, but she

79

was very close. The company had hired a new sales manager who had a real problem-accepting women in sales. He didn't want females in his department. Brenda was the only woman salesperson in her company.

The sales manager had made a conscious decision he would force Brenda out. She was trying to hold onto her position, but knew it was only a matter of time until he would be successful. He was determined she would go. Oh, he would give her another position in the company, but that position was meager and would mean a large cut in pay.

Her family room was not looking much better. A short time prior to our conversation she had gone through a bitter divorce. Like so many other married couples, their problems had accumulated over the years until finally everything exploded. Not only was it a bitter battle between them, but it was also very ugly. Her ex-husband decided he wanted their son, but not their daughter. This was one of those divorce cases where one parent who was filled with anger and hatred worked to turn a child against the other parent. That was the father's desire. Anytime her son was around her, he was abusive and hateful. Her daughter didn't understand what was happening. She was constantly upset, crying, and confused.

With these two rooms in disarray, you can imagine that her personal room was not a place she wanted to enter, much less spend time in. Whenever she found herself in her personal room, she didn't want to deal with the pressure there. Her personal room was filled with confusion and fear.

The only room left for her was the social room. Every Friday night she would get in her car and drive seventy miles to Minneapolis. She had to get away from St. Cloud. She told me that each time she went to Minneapolis she would visit a different nightspot, assume a new name and pretend she was someone new.

I'll always remember her words. "You may think I'm crazy," she said, "but this is the only way I can handle the pressure right now. If I don't get away, I'll come apart. My new identity allows me to escape from the pressure for just a little time."

I didn't think she was crazy. I had heard the same story so many times before.

When pressure is all consuming, it is only natural for us to run. When people find themselves in a tug-of-war, the typical person will seek an escape. The process of escape will normally take a person to the social room.

The relationship break-up scenario is so common. Whether it is the break-up of a marriage by divorce or the break-up of a dating relationship or the break-up of a friendship does not matter. People's lives will have vacancies in a room that has always been occupied. What do they do? They run to the social room looking for someone to fill the vacancy. They don't give themselves time to rearrange the fixtures that have been a part of their rooms for years. They don't allow time to heal. When they do this, whom do they attract? They attract another person just like the one who left. They place themselves in a position for the same thing to happen again, and that is usually what happens.

The loss of a job may also cause the need for escape. They can't believe it could happen to them! What are they going to do? That's usually not the first thought they have. The first thought is of a place they can go for sympathy. They sure can't go home for their desired sympathy. The home is in a state of panic. They will not go to the personal room. They

81

don't want to deal with the reality of the situation. That leaves them only one place to go—the social room. They know there they can find all the sympathy they want.

This philosophy is one I have found to be consistently true: *When people's lives have been devastated, they will go where they feel they can find agreement and/or sympathy.* They are not looking for help. They are looking for the right to grieve. They are looking for someone to say it really is terrible to have to go through what they are going through. They are looking for someone to validate their pain. They are looking for a friendly mourner. If other people disagree with them or their actions, they will go somewhere else. At this point they are not looking for help, but for agreement.

How many times have you seen the social room used as an escape? Have you ever wondered why there are so many gyms and workout clubs that are packed after the workday? Do you think that many people are really interested in their physical fitness? People walk into the social room so they do not have to visit another room. This creates pressure on them. They really aren't fooling themselves. They know why they are there. They know the game because they created the rules.

When the social room is used as an escape, it becomes a very dangerous room. When used as an escape, the occupant misses the real purpose of the room. The room is designed for relaxation and regrouping. The room should provide a release that prepares you to return with vigor to the other rooms.

Running to this room because you are running away from another room is not relaxation. If you're thinking, "At least in the social room I can let my hair down." The challenge with this reasoning is that you are not relaxing. You are only storing what will have to be faced. Outside you may be playing the

82

game, but inside you know the situation is still there waiting for you to handle it. You know you cannot stay in this room forever. You know you have to come out. That creates pressure.

What Your Social Room Should Do For You

When you use it correctly, the social room is a great room for controlling the stress in your life. Everyone needs a playroom! We all need a room where the child within us can come out and play. The child-like part of you is very important in controlling the stress in your life. It is the part that knows how to laugh, knows how to enjoy the simple things, and knows how to have fun with meaning.

The social room is a place where you can visit with other people. You need this interaction. You get interaction in the business room and family room, but normally that interaction is more intense. Most of the time, the interaction in the social room is more relaxed and informal. It is important to understand that the social room comes in many forms. There is the social drink with some friends; there is the golf or tennis game; there is the workout at the club; there is bridge or cards night; whatever wholesome fun you enjoy with friends.

This is definitely an important room for controlling the stress in your life. Again, the secret lies in the correct use of this room. Just as important as the correct use of the room is the kinds of people who occupy your social room with you. Realize that the people in this room can turn it into a room of pressure, rather than one of relaxation. There are three groups of people that share your social room with you: spectators, acquaintances and friends.

The Spectators

The spectators are people who do not help the stress in your life. They spend their energy offering you advice. They think they know what you should be doing in your situation. They have tons of advice and get upset if you don't use it. Spectators cannot be around you without needing to know what is going on in your life. They are a real drain, because they are constantly talking about your problems.

You must learn that these people do not relieve the pressure in your life; they create more pressure. They cannot help you because they do not really understand what you are going through. You must realize that this group is really nosey. All they are looking for is information they can use in their conversations with others about you. The more you tell them, the more they have to gossip about, and gossip they do! You have had to deal with spectators at various times in your life. Have you ever told someone something and had the information come back to you through a third party? You thought what you said would go no farther. When you asked them why they repeated the conversation to someone else, the response was either they did not say anything or they did not *remember* saying anything.

Spectators will always be part of your life. What you must learn is where to place these people and how much space to give them. Control them and they will simply be a presence. If you let them control you, they will become a source of stress.

The Acquaintances

You have more in common with acquaintances than you

do the spectators. You enjoy the time you spend with them. They know you, yet they do not know you, either. You let them into your life, but only so far. You like them, but you do not want them to know too much about you. Acquaintances make up the largest group of people in your social circle. That circle is important because it is the center of your relaxation. You can go out with acquaintances, let your hair down, laugh, enjoy yourself, and then carry on with your life. These people provide momentary release for you. That is their purpose in your life.

The Friends

The real special group of people in your social room are friends. They are also the smallest group in your social circle. The average human has no more than two friends at any one time. You will have many more spectators and acquaintances than friends.

Friends are different than spectators and acquaintances because they accept you as you are. They do not work to change you. They may give you advice, but when they do, you know it is because they care. Spectators and acquaintances are not this way; they offer advice because they want to change you. Most of the time their advice has a hidden agenda. Friends are very up-front. They say what they feel and leave it up to you to apply or reject their advice.

Friends do not demand your time. They are your friends whether you see them once a week or once a month. Spectators and acquaintances are different. They demand your time. If you go for a while without seeing them, they just won't see you any more.

85

Friends are relaxing to be around. You enjoy being with them. Not only do they provide a physical presence but a set of listening ears. Only with friends does real communication happen. Spectators and acquaintances provide a physical presence, but not a healthy set of ears. Spectators are good at providing a mouth. They want to talk, but not listen. Acquaintances will provide you with ears, but most of the time they do not really listen. That is one of the things that make acquaintances frustrating. Friends enjoy listening and sharing. Those friends in your life know more about you than anyone else. You tell them about your innermost thoughts, because you know you can trust them. You know they are there when you need them. The trust you have in them is an important release.

Use Your Social Room With Caution

Your social room is there to perform a necessary function and to provide you with a release from the pressures created in the other rooms of your life. It *is not* and *must not* become a room for escape. When that occurs, the purpose of this room is destroyed, and the room becomes a creator of pressure rather than a controller of pressure. Spend time in this room with meaning, and watch how it offers you the opportunity to regroup. When you use the social room correctly, you will find you are better prepared to face the other rooms in your life.

CHAPTER 8
The Personal Room

The smallest room in your four-room house is the personal room, but it's the most important room for your personal growth. The smallness of this room creates its weakness. The smaller the personal room, the greater the struggles are in the other rooms. You have to know who you are, and you will find this out only in your personal room.

You cannot lead another person
past the point where you are.

You cannot offer what you don't have. Your expertise comes from two areas:

1. *Things you have experienced and worked through yourself.*

2. *Situations you have walked through closely with other people.*

You've got to understand what the personal room is. This is the place and space where you go to be alone with you. If others go with you, it becomes a social room.

This room is where you disappear to spend time with you. It can be a bass boat, a wood working shop, a sitting room, or working in the yard. It can be a long walk, jogging, or working out in the gym. It is any space or place where you are alone with you.

Your growth has its origin in your personal room. It is in this room that you make the majority of the decisions that control your life. It is from your personal room that balance is given to the other rooms of your life.

People who are growth-oriented have large personal rooms. People who make a difference, both in their own lives and in the lives of others, have strong personal rooms.

People who are constantly struggling and are buried under the problems of life have very small personal rooms. The smaller the personal room, the less effective you are at controlling the pressures in life.

There are some truths concerning the personal room that you must understand. If you do not learn these, the personal room becomes a creator of stress, rather than a center of control.

What You Must Know About Your Personal Room

First, the personal room is an *alone room*. Life is a series of decisions. When those decisions are yours, but are made by others they will create pressure in your life.

My philosophy is this: I am alone. People look at me with questioning stares when I make that statement, but I feel that understanding it is a must for personal growth.

You see…I don't *need* people in order to be secure; I don't *need* people in order to have meaning for my life.

Here's my reasoning: If someone can give you happiness, they can also do what? They can take it away. If someone can give you security, they can also do what? They can take it away. If someone can create purpose for your life, they can also do what? They can destroy that purpose.

This almost sounds crazy, but if you want to screw up your life, fill it with people you *need*. If I need you, what do I do with you? I place restrictions upon you. I live with blinders on and only look at you through my needs. What happens if you do not meet my needs? I criticize you. If you do not meet my needs, I look for someone who will.

The secret is to *want*, not *need*. If I *want* you, I accept you as you are. If I *want* you, I take away the restrictions. I turn you loose and let you be what you were meant to be in my life.

Want is created through personal strength. *Need* is created through personal weakness. *Want* is the controlling force only when I am secure within myself. When I am not comfortable with me, I *need* people.

When you *want* people, you work to understand them; when you *need* people, you use them. When you *want* people you focus on their strengths; when you *need* people you point out their weaknesses.

I am alone. Personal growth is a personal responsibility. If I depend upon others to do what is my responsibility, I set myself up to experience disappointment, rejection, despair, and pressure. Whether you like it or not, you are alone.

Have you ever met people who are always asking others what they should do? They never seem to handle a situation by themselves. They need others to decide for them. What happens if advice they are given does not work? Who do they blame? Somehow, these people seem to feel this creates less pressure. People who spend their lives needing other people place more pressure on themselves. When you need others, they must always be there. If they are not, there are feelings of panic and of being lost.

Need is a trap that is taught in childhood. Parents work to make their children dependent, rather than independent by doing everything for them including making decisions. One day these children have to face the real world, and they are not prepared.

Once when I was in Daytona Beach to speak, I went to the hotel restaurant one morning for breakfast. I could not help but overhear the conversation-taking place at the next table. This young boy was there to register for college. When his parents informed him that they were going to drop him off at campus, run some errands, and then pick him up later in the day, he was not agreeable. He needed them to go with him. He didn't know what to do. If they weren't going with him, he was not going.

When he went to the restroom, the father said to the mother, *"You have really ruined that kid. I've told you for years to stop doing everything for him, but no—you had to do everything. Look at him now."*

I thought to myself… "another dependent." Growth occurs through one's ability to *want* more than to *need.* That can only occur when you understand the necessity for accepting "I am alone."

Another concept you must know about your personal room is: *everything in it is original.* For some people the personal room is a struggle, because there they cannot pretend. Many people spend their lives pretending that what is *not,* really *is.* As long as they can stay away from the personal room, they can play their games. Alone in the personal room, they must deal with reality.

It is hard for these people to find their originality. They are caught up in being liked, being accepted, and they will do anything to make those things happen. They don't understand the pressure this creates. Pretense is a crippling game of constant pressure. Pretense results in a self-imposed sentence of low self-esteem. Pretense is an illusion that may create momentary escape, but at the same time it creates pressure for tomorrow.

The more you like *you*, the more you fight to be an original. The more of an original you are, the more control you exercise over your life. The more of an original you strive to become, the less dependent you are on others. The more you work to be an original, the more you will find yourself in the personal room.

You have to absolutely, positively remember that the personal room is PERSONAL.

It is important to understand that others may share in your life, but they must not consume you. I'm sure you've met the "smothering personality" type. That person must always be around you. That person must always know where you are, where you are going, what you are thinking…that person wants to know everything. That's pressure for both of you.

Your life needs some privacy. Your life needs a corner that is neither filled with nor invaded by others. The personal room is *your* personal room. It is the room in your house where you can keep personal things. It is a room in your life you do not have to share with others. It should be the room where you can go to visit with yourself.

The growth in your life originates and is given stability in the personal room.

The more quality time you spend in the personal room, the more growth-oriented your life will be. The larger you allow this room to become, the more stability you will have for the other three rooms of your life.

You might think it's absurd to teach people to spend vast amounts of time in this room. Maybe you think that much time is not necessary. The reality is this: *the more quality time you spend in the personal room the more creativity and control you have for the other rooms.*

The Stressors

The personal room has its own unique creators of stress. The more you understand these, the more control you will have for the other rooms.

The first stressor in your personal room is a *lack of alone time.* Most people who walk through the front door of your life need (and expect) you to give them time and energy. The more your world is filled with giving energy to others, the more alone time you require.

On the days when everyone is pulling at you it's natural to want to run away, but what if there was no place to go. It is amazing how people can be so demanding of your energy, isn't it? They think you never get tired. They treat you as an endless reservoir of energy. The more you give, the more they demand.

To control stress, you must control the energy drains. To control stress, you must have alone time. Other people will not give you alone-time. You must schedule and take time for yourself. Remember, you cannot give to others what you don't have.

The second stressor in this room is a *lack of respectful, listening ears.* Have you ever had a day when you wanted someone to listen and all they wanted to do was talk? Isn't it interesting how everyone needs to talk, but few want to listen? How many times have you been in a conversation with someone and listened as the individual went on and on about a lot of nothing? This person finishes the verbal assault, and you think—now it's my time. Then, what does the other person do? They leave!

How many times have you wanted to just talk without having the other party respond with solutions and opinions? Many people cannot listen without offering advice.

It may be difficult to find respectful, listening ears. Have you ever kept something inside of you because you could not find a set of respectful, listening ears?

Each person requires a special someone who is willing to listen respectfully. To control the pressure in your life, you must find those respectful, listening ears. To control the stress in your life, you must have those ears that you can invite into your life for a chat.

Our next stressor in the personal room is the *loss of a challenge.* The personal room is where you create, define, and design your dreams. As long as you have a dream, your life has motivation and a challenge. A challenge is a doorway into tomorrow. A challenge is mental nourishment. A challenge is emotional fuel.

If your life loses its challenge, it loses its direction. When the challenge is lost, so is the desire.

In the personal room you must constantly review your dream. You must know whether the dream is still accurate. You must know whether the dream is still what you want for your life.

It is possible for a dream to get buried under clutter and be replaced by a fantasy. When a dream gets buried and is not re-defined, it continues to exist as a fantasy. When this happens, you can continue to put energy into it, but the result will be negative. Energy will be expended, but not replaced. Action will occur, but without a definable direction. Physically you may be there, but mentally and emotionally you will disappear.

Your life needs a challenge. Without it you will wander around full of despair and frustration. It is vital that you continually review your dream.

Several years ago, I spoke at a convention in Wisconsin. Later in the evening, the entire group went on a dinner cruise on the most magnificent riverboat you have ever seen. I was on the top deck enjoying the sights and sounds when the executive vice-president of the association approached me.

He grabbed my attention when he said, "You weren't too kind to me today."

I wasn't sure what he was saying, but he needed to talk, so I prepared myself to listen.

"I've been the executive vice-president of this group for twenty-six years. That's a long time to work with one group. The past four years have been extremely tough on me. You see…I really don't want to do this anymore. I get up almost every morning and dread going to work. I know you are wondering why I stay. I only have three more years until I retire. If I leave this job, where would I go? Who would hire me? I can't leave this group and have the financial package I have here. I'm the perfect example of what you were talking about. I've lost my dream, my challenge, and my desire. I really don't know what to do."

What pressure there was for him! When your life has a challenge, it has a means of developing positive stress. If your life loses the challenge, stress becomes a negative force.

The next stressor in the personal room is *fear of failure*. In the personal room you create the beliefs and thoughts that go with you to the other rooms. The actions that occur in the other rooms are given their meaning in the personal room. It is here you make the decision whether you can or you can't. The visualization of that decision will be seen in the other rooms involved, but the decision is made in the personal room.

People who are given tasks that they do not think they can complete will ultimately fail. Their belief that they could not do it destroyed their creative ability. They defined a plan of failure and set out to accomplish it.

This statement is huge: the *real* you, not the you that most people know, but the *real* you, lives in the personal room. In this room, pretense breaks down. Here, understandings are formed. Here you decide, design, and formulate what will happen in the other rooms of your life.

The fear of failure is a crippling disease when it controls you. This fear is a crossroad in the human life. It is natural. When a human life must face a challenge, there will always be an element of fear.

Some people take the fear and turn it into creative energy. They do not let fear create an imaginary monster. *Fear can be food for creativity.*

Others take the same fear and turn it into a negative force. Fear becomes a wall they cannot scale. Rather than producing a creative climate, the fear creates a real monster defined by the words "I can't." When these words write the script, defeat is an impending doom.

It is in the personal room you define your self-image. It is in the personal room your thoughts are given visual scripts. It is in the personal room that you define your tomorrow.

95

Learn this: fear is pressure, but it does not have to be destructive. Replace the thought of failure with the desire to succeed, and the stress nurtures growth.

There is one other stressor to be mentioned here. It is the *lack of flexibility*. Contrary to popular belief, most people are stubborn. Do you remember what was said in the very beginning of this book? People live their lives in an effort to establish comfortable routines. Routine lacks flexibility and adaptability.

Your personal room is the room for decisions. If you lack flexibility, there will be tremendous pressure. The most constant part of life is change. The lack of flexibility is a refusal to accept change as a step toward improvement. Change is life's way of redecorating. The lack of flexibility is a way of keeping the interior decorator out.

When change is necessary but denied, the result will be frustration and negative stress. Flexibility is a must for controlling the stress in the personal room.

What Your Personal Room Means To Your Life

Your personal room is undoubtedly the most important room in your house. It is from this room that meaning is defined. It is from this room that you create your mental and emotional preparation for all that occurs in the other rooms.

As long as the personal room is the smallest room in your house, you do not have a chance of controlling the stress in your life. The ability to control it will be discovered as your personal room goes through renovation and expansion. The construction will begin only when you can take an honest look at what is and become comfortable going into this room with the real you. When that desire is greater than the desire to pretend, your personal room will grow!

CHAPTER 9
The Stress-Prone Personality

Sometimes we are just our own worst enemy. Some of us just worry about worrying!

As long as I live, I'll never forget Mark. Mark was one of my students at Ohio University. He was really a nice kid, but one who worried about every step he took. He worried about everything—the Rice Krispie that didn't go pop, the little toad that hopped too quickly, the chicken that wasn't (because he ate the egg at breakfast)—he worried about all the unimportant things in life!

One day, Mark came to my office and asked me if I knew of any books that had been written about "worry" that might help him. I had a book in my library entitled, How To Win Over Worry. After a long conversation I convinced him to take the book and read it. One hour and fifteen minutes later Mark was back in my office with the book. I said, "Mark, you sure didn't waste any time reading the book. What did you think of it?"

His reply was a classic. He said, "Oh, I haven't read it yet. I was so afraid I would lose it I thought I'd better bring it back. How about me sitting here and reading it? That way I won't worry about losing it."

There are people who don't have to seek stress...they *are* stress. Not only are they their own worst enemy, but they also can destroy *you* just by being around them. They can turn sunshine into a rainstorm even when there are no clouds in the sky.

97

Many people are their own worse enemy.

Uncontrolled stress is not an accident; it's an invitation that is issued. It's not an event, but a reaction to an event. It's a loss of control over a situation to the point where the situation controls the person.

There is a very real thing called the stress-prone personality. There are certain personality traits that, when spotted, help you know you are or are not working with a stressful person. Drawing from the research of Dr. Rosalind Forbes[5], let's look at her theory of stress-prone people.

The Ten Personality Traits of Stress-Prone People[5]

The first characteristic of the self-destructive personality is a *tendency to over plan each day*. This is the sixty-hour a week person. This is the person who plans, and plans, but gets further and further behind. This is the person who pushes himself to the point of trying to be superhuman. These people think they can accomplish more than anyone else. Their time is so planned that any unplanned interruption causes a total disaster.

The typical behavioral pattern of this person is striving to fit as many things as possible into the time span that has been allotted. Then comes the realization that there is not enough time, so the big push comes to try to make everything fit. Realizing the problem, the over planner will still do the same thing tomorrow.

Have you ever seen over planners? They're whirlwinds. Every time you see them, they're moving at an unmanageable pace. If you try to find out what they are accomplishing, you cannot; yet, they are busy.

The second characteristic is *polyphasic thinking*. These people seldom live in the world where they are and think many different thoughts at the same time. They cannot live with one thought, but are constantly working on multiple ideas.

It is not unusual to find these people eating a meal while simultaneously reading the paper or a book, listening to the radio, and planning the afternoon and evening. If someone speaks, they may appear to be listening, but are actually thinking of several other things.

These people may seem to have many friendships, but it is not surprising to find that few are deep and meaningful.

You think you know this type of personality until you really have time to sit down and talk. Then you realize they are all "show."

The third characteristic of the self-destructive personality is *the need to win*. These people must win at everything they do. They can't be happy if they do not win. The impulse to win is so strong that many times even a game with a child can turn into a battle. Winning is the most important thing in the world to them.

Do you know any of these win-or-die personalities? The drive to be number one overrides everything else. They will do almost anything to win a contest. They are constantly using other people to win at whatever they are doing.

The next characteristic is *the persistent desire for advancement or recognition*. While it is natural for all humans to want recognition for a job well done or advancement to a position for which they feel qualified, stress-prone people become hostile and angry when they do not receive such recognition. Their persistent desire for recognition pervades everything they do.

Individuals with this trait are concerned with accruing material wealth or possessions as proof of success. Money often becomes symbolic of achievement; however, these people seldom enjoy the fruits of their labors because of the time-crunch they have created.

On the surface, these people seem to be extremely confident and self-assured. Underneath, basic feelings of insecurity may be the prime motivation for seeking outside recognition and taking on outside work. Their concern is primarily with achieving a goal, only to take on another goal once the last one has been accomplished. They believe achievements prove their worth to their peers. The adoration and approval of peers are things that they must obtain.

This personality type is compelled to live a life that seldom brings inner contentment or peacefulness. This will be the case as long as value and worth are measured by things, rather than by inner traits.

Have you met these people? They are the ones always calling attention to themselves. They will not let anything they do go unnoticed. They see plaques, awards, and vocal recognition as the way of saying who they are, rather than letting their true self speak.

The fifth characteristic of the self-destructive personality is *the inability to relax without feeling guilty.* To this personality type time is for "doing" and not "enjoying." Every moment must be filled with accomplishment. Any activity that is not work is seen as wasteful. To this personality even sleep can be a time of work. This person dreams about things that need to be done or about how to accomplish a certain task. This personality always feels tired because time is for doing, and there is a feeling of guilt when productivity is at a standstill.

Have you met this person? Always uptight—always giving off a feeling of tension and unease and never learning the value of meditation. This person cannot understand the need to stop long enough to allow his or her body to regroup to move on in a positive manner.

The sixth characteristic of the self-destructive personality is *impatience with delays or interruptions*. This personality has not learned to roll with the punches. Everyone else must meet their schedules and deadlines. Their way of doing something is the only way. If things are not done their way, then criticism abounds. Fault is always with the other person.

This attitude carries over into every area of life. This personality always pushes everyone else. The pace must be theirs, or they just cannot be included. If this happens, they must accept the criticism for not being "with it."

Have you met this person with never enough time for you? You feel like you have to run instead of walk to keep up with them. This person is constantly "short" in dealing with people. When you ask a question, you are made to feel as though you were imposing.

The seventh characteristic of the self-destructive personality is *involvement in multiple projects with many deadlines*. This personality has the tendency to overextend his involvement. These people will be involved in as many activities as they can cram into their lives. Many of these activities will not be job-related. This creates fragmentation and frustration. It is interesting because with deadlines, frustration, and fragmentation there can be very little, if any, pleasure derived from the involvement.

Dr. Forbes makes the point that people with this trait are "their own worst enemy." Because they overextend themselves with too many projects and activities, their creativity and judgment are greatly reduced and they tend to make more errors. In essence, they become, "one man bands" in their quest to accomplish so many things in the time allotted.

Have you ever met these people? They must be a part of everything that is going on. No meeting or function can take place without them. They constantly volunteer for anything that needs to be done. Their name is known because of their involvement in everything.

The eighth characteristic of the self-destructive personality *is a chronic sense of time urgency.* To these people, time is always an enemy. Time causes a constant wrestling match. Time is a source of stress because it controls them, instead of them controlling it. This causes them to constantly create deadlines that may not exist.

Have you met these people? They live on the run. They cannot walk between meetings because time would be wasted and schedules are so close. Running is the only way to make it. You can easily recognize these people. They walk in late, knowing you will understand; they were tied up in another meeting.

The ninth characteristic of the self-destructive personality *is an excessive competitive drive.* Competition has built the American economy. Competition, within its correct structure, is healthy. People with this personality have taken competition out of context and turned something healthy into a disease. This competitive spirit naturally forces this personality type to constantly perform. It creates restlessness and discontentment. These people cannot be happy with their accomplishments, because they are already focused on the next task. As long as another person has a larger piece of the pie, they won't be satisfied.

Have you met these people? They thrive on competition. They cannot be happy unless they are involved in a competitive struggle with others. For this personality type, life is a battle involving numbers, output, and achievements.

The final characteristic of the self-destructive personality is *compulsion to overwork—this is the workaholic.* To this person work is their life. They are blinded to anything taking place around them that does not pertain to work.

Do you know any workaholics? They are the first to arrive at the office and the last to leave. They live, eat, and breathe their work. Everything around them—recreation, exercise, family and friends—suffers because of their work.

I once heard an interview by Christopher J. Hegarty, an authority on job stress. He gave a brief Workaholic Quiz. See how you fair:

1. *Do you regularly take office work home at night or over the weekend?*

2. *Are you reluctant to go on vacation for fear things at the office will go wrong?*

3. *Do you take phone calls even when trying to complete a difficult job or relax on a coffee break?*

4. *Do you ask others to put in the same hours as you?*

5. *Do you avoid delegating work because you feel you're the only one who can do it right?*

6. *Is your desk so piled with paperwork that often you couldn't find things?*

103

7. *Are you an obsessive memo writer?*

According to Mr. Hegarty, a "yes" answer to more than three of these makes you a workaholic.

You Know You Best!

No one knows you better than you know yourself. Sure, it's difficult to be honest with yourself about your traits, but your life depends upon it. You can be your own worst enemy. Does your personality lend itself to stress? Let's carry on and see what kind of changes you can make in your life that will help you control your stress.

A Stress-Prone Personality Questionnaire*

DIRECTIONS: Rate yourself as to how you typically react in each of these situations. There are no right or wrong answers.

4—Always   3—Frequently   2—Sometimes   1—Never

_____ Do you try to do as much as possible in the least amount of time?

_____ Do you always have to win at games to enjoy yourself?

_____ Do you find yourself speeding up the car to beat the red light?

_____ Are you unlikely to ask for or indicate your need for help with a problem?

_____ Do you constantly seek the respect and admiration of others?

_____ Are you overly critical of the way others do their work?

_____ Do you have the habit of looking at your watch or clock often?

_____ Do you constantly strive to better your position and achievements?

_____ Do you spread yourself "too thin" in terms of your time?

continued...

_____ Do you have a habit of doing more than one thing at a time?

_____ Do you frequently get angry or irritable?

_____ Do you have little time for hobbies or time by yourself?

_____ Do you have a tendency to talk quickly or hasten conversations?

_____ Do you consider yourself hard-driving?

_____ Do you have a tendency to get involved in multiple projects?

_____ Do you have a lot of deadlines in your work?

_____ Do you feel vaguely guilty if you relax and do nothing during leisure?

_____ Do you take on too many responsibilities?

_____ TOTAL SCORE

SCORE KEY:

If your score is between 20-30, chances are you are non-productive and your life lacks stimulation.

If your score is between 31-50, you have good balance in your ability to handle and control stress.

If your score is between 51-60, your stress line is on a fence. You must make some changes.

If your score is 61-Over, Get Professional Help!

Life Stress by Dr. Rosalind Forbes

CHAPTER 10
Guidelines For Stress Management

A woman came to me after I had finished a seminar and wanted to talk. She was like so many people I have met. It wasn't that she didn't know what her problem was; it was that she didn't know what to do about it. Her life had been so simple until a few months ago when her husband was killed in an automobile accident. She had never had to make any major decisions. He had always been her strength. Now she didn't have him for support and guidance.

She looked at me with eyes filled with pain and confusion and said, *"You can't believe the pressure on me. The farm has to be run; the children need my time; the other business endeavors need my energy; and my own career is now on hold."*

She paused for a moment and then continued, *"There is not enough of me to go around. I can't be all things to all people."*

Then she looked down, looked around, and continued, *"I'm not doing too well. My pressure gauge has been in the red for almost a year now. I have to do something."*

Most people can live under pressure—under stress. You do it everyday. Everything is okay as long as you feel you are in control of the way you are handling the pressure. Then when the bells sound; the alarms go off, and you realize you are no longer in control; you have an emotional faucet you can't turn off. When you are honest enough to admit what is happening, you start looking for help. Recovery is so much easier if you deal with matters when you notice the warning signs. You must learn to recognize when your pressure gauge

109

is moving into the red zone. You must know when to start turning the pressure valve down. The sooner you admit it — the sooner you are honest — the sooner you will start releasing the pressure.

The hardest thing about what I do is trying to "generalize" it for the masses. Your stress is different than anyone else's stress. I am about to give you some guidelines for controlling your stress, but you will have to adapt these to your specific stress in your unique life. These guidelines for successful stress management are the keys to keeping the pressure under control.

Before you start working through these guidelines, let's get a picture of how the stress enters your life because it will help you know why you react the way you do.

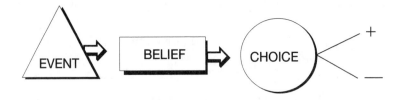

Your life is made up of events. Every situation you have experienced or are experiencing is of major importance. Every event, no matter how insignificant it may seem, is writing the script for your today and your tomorrow.

The events take on even more importance when you understand that with each event you have a belief about what that event means to you. You have feelings about every single thing that goes on in your life. Some feelings are stronger than others. Beliefs are your emotional thoughts that surround the events.

These beliefs, your emotional thoughts that surround the events, create choices. The choice, the decision you make, is the result of your beliefs—*not the result of the event.* People share common events, but make different choices, because their beliefs are different.

Pressure or stress is not created because of the events in your life. The pressure is created from the beliefs you hold about those events. The choice can either add to or take away from the pressure.

You must remember you cannot eliminate the events. They will occur. You must work on controlling your beliefs. The more you control your emotional thoughts that surround the events, the more you can control the pressure.

These guidelines are not magical. They are simply suggestions that you must interpret according to where you are in your personal development. DO NOT work on all of them at the same time! Choose the guidelines that deal with where you are now and start with those. The others you may see as not being valuable right now, but you shouldn't totally disregard them. Remember, you are changing, and what doesn't fit you today may fit tomorrow!

Guidelines To Manage Your Stress

Guideline #1:
Don't Be Afraid To Take A Risk

A man came to me wanting help, so we sat for two hours and talked. When we were finished, we had discovered he had more options than he had first realized. As he sat and thought through them, he finally told me that they were all too risky. He didn't understand the difference between a *risk* and a *gamble. A gamble is a decision you make when you have not taken enough time to gather the necessary information, or you have not put enough mental energy into determining the probable results.* Gambling creates pressure because you have very little information, if any, on which to base your decision.

A risk is different. There is still pressure, but of a different kind. *A risk is a decision you make that is based on adequate thought and research.* It is a decision you make in a situation where you can almost predict the end result.

Risk pressure is created by the sheer process of making a decision, but it is controlled by research and thought. *Gambling pressure* is created by the lack of knowledge and thought and it increases with each aspect of the situation you face.

Don't be afraid to be a risk-taker. That's pressure you can control. You know what is because you examined the possibilities. Don't live your life as a gambler. Don't live your life making decisions while wearing blinders. There will always be decisions for you to make, and within every decision is a right and wrong answer. Do the research, think through and seek the solution, rather than feed the confusion.

Guideline #2:
Turn Every Obstacle Or Problem Into A
Creative Growth Experience

This is us in a perfect world! I live with the philosophy *every situation in life is a gift.* The gift is given for positive growth. That positive growth can only be discovered as you search through the event and collect what you believe to be the value of the experience. If all you can see in the event is the destructive part, that's all you will take away from it. On the other hand, if you can recognize the negative, but focus on the strengths of the event, that's what you will take away.

There is positive value in every event in your life. Sometimes you have to look for it, and that's the challenge. Some people love to wallow in their misery. They don't want to discover the good. If they focused on the good, they couldn't hold onto their pain. I really believe people who are always seeking the bad are people crying out for attention. They don't realize the pressure they place on themselves. Dealing with the bad takes more energy and creates more pressure than dealing with the situation as it is and moving on with understanding of what happened!

Learn to discover the value of life's events, and you will learn to relieve your pressure. It is not always easy, but it is possible. Every situation in life is a gift. It's given to you to unwrap and use for healthy growth!

Guideline #3:
Make Conscious Decisions

Do you have someone in your life that asks your opinion about all the decisions they must make? These are people wanting you (and probably others) to make decisions for them. Life is not to be designed by other people drawing your road map. When others are writing the script for your life, you become an actor in someone else's play. No one has the right to write your script. You must make your own decisions. When others decide for you, then you become what *they* want you to be.

Have confidence in yourself. Believe in your abilities and talents. Understand that no one knows you better than you know yourself. Don't become a puppet for anyone. Make decisions based upon *your* wishes, *your* knowledge, and *your* thoughts. You can seek other's advice, but define it in light of what *you* want, not what *they* need you to be.

You can't remove the pressure of decision-making by letting others make decisions for you. When others are controlling you, more pressure is created. When *you* make the decisions, you are in control. Make conscious decisions!

Guideline #4:
Don't Be Afraid To Make Mistakes

The fear of making a mistake is the downfall of many people. They will not act for fear they will do something wrong. It's amazing how many people live under the pressure caused by the fear of making a mistake.

I met a man on an airplane who was very intriguing to me. He was a dreamer. He was interested in what I did professionally and in the fact that my business had grown so rapidly. The more he talked about his dreams, the more frustrated he became. I finally asked him why he didn't stop what he was doing and go after his dream. He wasn't happy with his life the way it was. His response was typical: he was afraid it wouldn't work.

What pressure people place on themselves when they are afraid to try because they might make a mistake! They really want to try, but fear controls them.

I was acquainted with a young couple once that will never know what kind of a life they could have had. They got along well; they enjoyed so many of the same things; they loved each other. The day came when they needed to make a decision about their future. She wanted to marry him, but because of a past relationship experience she considered a mistake, she was afraid. The fear of her past was controlling her present and her future. She pushed him away and missed what that relationship could have been to her life.

You must believe that you cannot base all of your decisions on what has happened. You must know that mistakes will happen. You cannot avoid making them. To live avoiding mistakes is to live in a shelter with no exit door. Don't be afraid to make mistakes! It's through mistakes that you will grow. Mistakes will constantly remind you that you are human. It is important you remember that mistakes are a one-time happening. If you repeat the same behavior that created the mistake, it is no longer a mistake; it has become your plan.

Guideline #5:
Set Priorities

For some people deciding what to do is very difficult. They have so many projects going they don't know where to start. They have a hard time defining priorities because everything must be done. One of the most important thoughts concerning priorities is *"there is only one of me."* You can only do so much. When you spread yourself so thin that you wind up as the maintenance director of your life rather than as the president, it causes you increased pressure.

One man was a nervous wreck by the time he got to me. In his hand he had a list of things to do. He threw it down on the table and said, *"Look at this! There are thirty things on the list for me to do. I can't get them all done. I find myself so concerned with what I'm not doing, I won't get anything done."*

Sound familiar? Many times our problem isn't in knowing *what* to do; it is in knowing *where* to start. Priorities are determined by the flow of energy from you in your life.

115

When you can determine what is taking your energy, you can determine your priorities. You may think you have your priorities in order, but study the energy flow. What are you really doing? What you are doing is your real priority.

Here's something else to consider: nobody can tell you what is important. You are the only person that can make that decision. *Priority is your understanding of what you need to do and when you need to do it.* When you plan your energy flow to the events in your life, you not only understand priority, but you also control the pressure.

Guideline #6:
If You Find Yourself In A Rut, Change Your Routine

One fact people do not pay enough attention to is sameness. When your life is so predictable that there is no newness, pressure is created. Newness creates growth; growth spurs creativity; creativity keeps life from getting into a rut.

It was once said the difference between a grave and a rut is *a rut is a grave with both ends kicked out.* It's easy for life to slip into a rut. You become so familiar with what you are doing you don't have to put any thought into the action. That creates the frustration with situations, which in turn creates pressure.

You know yourself well enough to know when you're digging a rut. When you discover it, don't let it persist. Change the habit—the routine. Don't allow sameness to bury you!

Guideline #7:
Form A Mental Picture Of The "You" Who You Would Like To Be And Work On Becoming That "You"

She was like so many of the people I meet each day. As I listened to her talk, all she did was put herself down. She didn't like the person she was, but she was not trying to do anything about it, either.

When you do not like what you see, you put a lot of pressure on yourself. It's okay to be honest as long as the honesty is not turned into a personal beating.

You become what you see yourself as. Each of us paints a self-portrait and lives that portrait out in real life everyday. You must paint a portrait of what you *want* to be. The painting must be real, not a fantasy. When you can paint that true painting, you will be amazed at how you work to become the image you have created.

It may not be easy, but don't get discouraged. Admit your weaknesses, and focus on your strengths. You will find the more you focus on your strengths, the stronger you will become, and in your strengths those weaknesses cannot control your picture of life.

Guideline #8:
Evaluate Your Present Work Or Job

It's amazing how many people are not honest concerning their feelings about their jobs. They will do it for years—get up each morning, hating what they do, yet never be honest about their feelings.

You must constantly evaluate what you're doing with your life. If the direction of your life is filled with frustration, you will find yourself struggling with pressure. How long has it been since you honestly evaluated how you feel about your present job? Does it still make you happy? Are you still excited about the work? Is there anything you could do that

would bring you a greater sense of happiness? Do you believe
enough in your talents and abilities to run with your dream?

I met a gentleman on an Air Canada flight to Fredericton,
New Brunswick. We were chatting about our lives when he
began to open up. He was an engineer who worked for the
Canadian government. He had a very secure job. In just
fifteen more years, he could retire. For the last ten years,
each morning he had gotten up, gone to work, and with each
new day hated it more and more. He had had a dream, but
the years of going to a job that was no longer fulfilling had
emotionally exhausted him. Finally, the pressure got to
him. He could feel his whole life coming apart. He made an
important discovery—*what good is security if you don't enjoy
what you are doing?* He went home and announced to his wife
he was going to reach for his dream. He was amazed at how
supportive she was. I heard from him a year later. Now he's
fulfilling his dream. There is still pressure, but this pressure is
fun!

Evaluation should cause growth. Don't be afraid to be
honest concerning the way you feel about what you are doing.
Don't be afraid to challenge your routine!

Guideline #9:
Keep the Balance Between
Too Little And Too Much Stress

Earlier I stated that if you took all the stress out of your
life, you would die. I also said that if you have too much stress
in your life, it can destroy you. The secret is not to eliminate
the stress, but to control it.

You know yourself better than anyone. You know when
you are under too much pressure. When you realize it, don't

create more pressure by trying to eliminate it. Bring things under control. You will then have things in perspective and be able to make the best decisions.

Guideline #10:
Learn To Relax

Relaxing is a difficult thing for many people to do. Sometimes when you think you are relaxing, you are continuing to work. *Relaxation is the ability to turn your mind off and give it the freedom to go wherever it wants to go.* Relaxation is the body in a restful state. Some people find this difficult to achieve. Not only do you have to know *when* to relax, but also *how* to relax.

Relaxation takes different forms for different people. Some women can relax by going shopping, or cleaning, or reading a book. Some men can relax by working in the yard, or fishing, or getting involved in sports. Some relax by doing nothing. You must find whatever it is that takes your body from a pressured state to a restful state. Learn to relax!

Guideline #11:
Don't Allow Criticism To Stop You

When Dori came to me, she was so frustrated she was in tears. She said, "No matter what I do they criticize me. Why do they do that? It makes me not want to do anything."

How many people have you known who did not accomplish something (or maybe did not even start it) for fear of being criticized? You must not let criticism stop you.

You must understand the psychology of criticism. Criticism is never positive. It is an emotional attack on a person who is generally not present. Most criticism is created out of jealousy and/or envy. Any time you are accomplishing someone's dream before that person can accomplish it, you will see some jealousy. Any time you find one person threatened by another, you will generally find jealousy. That jealousy will surface in the form of criticism. Recognize it and don't let criticism stop you!

Guideline #12:
Work Toward Your Dream

When a person stops growing and reaches a place where their life is just "happening," then that person will have stress. Everyone needs a time of suspended movement, but only a short time. If growth is not resumed, you will experience depression, anger, over-reaction to what others say, withdrawal, and other symptoms of stress.

It is important you have a creative plan of growth for your life. This means you must plan dreams for your life. If I've heard it once, I have heard it a hundred times... "My problem is I have no dream for my life." Show me a person who has lost their dream, and I'll show you a person whose life is not growing.

Ask yourself these questions: "What am I doing to improve myself or my work? Am I working toward my dream? Am I reaching for a positive dream? Do I have a defined direction?"

Guideline #13:
Don't Let Things Drift

You create tension by procrastinating...putting off things that need to be done. You think you always have tomorrow, then suddenly the unexpected happens, and there is too much for you to do. The result is uncontrollable stress.

The challenge is one of organization. You must have a system of organization. You work, but with no real plan. You will find you can control a lot of pressure if you don't let things drift. Organize in your mind what needs to be done, make a checklist, and then attack the list. The amount of free time you will have when you learn to do things in an organized fashion is amazing.

Guideline #14:
Acknowledge Your Fears

Fear can create an enormous amount of pressure. It sits in the corner of your life like a predator just waiting to attack you. You know it is there, but you choose to pretend it does not exist. Then, all of a sudden it attacks!

We have been conditioned to see fear as a weakness. Did you know that everyone has fears? *Fear is only a weakness when you do not deal with it.* Leave it alone, and it will take creative strength from you.

Acknowledge your fears. When you admit to your fears, you begin to turn them into creative growth. Once you acknowledge them, your creativity will allow you to deal with them constructively.

Guideline #15:
Don't Blame Others

Some people cannot accept responsibility for anything they do. If something is wrong, it is never their fault. It is easier to find someone else to blame. These are people who have never learned that responsibility carries with it both praise and fault. When people in roles of leadership or management cannot accept blame, they are defining their lack of qualification for those positions.

To pass blame takes a lot of energy. It creates pressure added to the fear the situation has already created. That can be controlled by letting the responsibility fall where it should.

Guideline #16:
Don't Compromise Who You Are

I cannot begin to tell you the number of people who create pressure in their lives by compromising who they are. You can get so caught up in trying to do or be what others want you to be, you lose sight of the "Real You."

Don't compromise who you are! If others cannot accept you as you are, then realize it is their loss.

Do you understand why so many people are willing to compromise? Some people are so lonely for companionship they will do anything for acceptance. Others are so insecure with themselves they allow those around them to write the scripts for their lives. They know the frustration and pressure of compromise, but compromise provides a sense of security. Compromising yourself is never a good idea! It makes you an actor in someone else's play.

Guideline #17:
Do Something For Others

A life that does not have room for others is a pressure cooker. People who live with the "I" philosophy generally live in fear of others.

I'll never forget a wealthy Texan I met. Roy was wealthy, yet had nothing inwardly. He lived with the attitude that everyone wanted something from him. He had no friends, because friends were people who only wanted to be close enough to use him.

I sat and listened to Roy's philosophies and walked away feeling sorry for him. He had never learned the true meaning of the gift of people. One of the greatest rewards in life is the involvement you can have with others. The more you share with others, the more you will grow. The more you give of yourself, the more you will have to give. The more you give of yourself, the more you will receive.

Guideline #18:
Arrange For Privacy

The more I see of our fast-paced society the more I believe that one of the greatest creators of pressure is the lack of quality alone time.

On a very crowded flight I overheard a flight attendant say, *"I have to get away! I can't take another request or complaint! Do you mind if I lock myself in the restroom for a few minutes?"*

Have you ever been ready to explode because of the crowds in your life? Or do you just need that personal space to regroup for even a few minutes?

Everyone needs privacy. You need time when there is no one in your world, but you. Have you noticed if you don't arrange for it, it doesn't happen? You have to plan for it and protect it.

Guideline #19:
Don't Overdo A Problem

You rate the problems in your life by the amount of emotional and mental energy you give them. Some you don't give enough energy; others you give too much.

I became acquainted with a man who was really struggling with a personal relationship...struggling to the point that the situation was receiving all of his mental and emotional energy. This one situation was destroying him. There was nothing to his life but this situation! Pressures were being exerted from other directions, but he just stacked them on top. The weight became so heavy he almost broke.

You need to learn you can put *so much* energy into a situation that it destroys your ability to work effectively. Overdoing a problem can destroy the creative part of you that really holds the answer. When you learn to control the "emotional you," then the "logical you" will help direct your energy.

Guideline # 20:
Make Timely Decisions

Over-thinking can cause pressure. When you have a decision to make and wrestle with it for a length of time, there is pressure. Remember, you already know what to do. Most of the time you know the decision you need to make; you just live with the fear of making it! The fear of decision is another pressure creator.

One day I ran into a lady whom I had met several days earlier. We had talked the first day, but it was only idle chatter. This day was different because she needed a friend. She was married, but she felt the marriage had been dead for more than a year. As I listened to her talk, it became evident she had mentally and emotionally divorced her husband some time ago. She just hadn't been able to make the decision to actually take action to get the legal divorce. She was fearful of what it would do to others around her. She had made the decision, but fear kept her from putting physical action to that which she had already mentally and emotionally decided. The unneeded stress was pulling her apart.

The pressure from decision doesn't come from making the decision, but from implementing the decision. Don't let decisions hang. When you know the outcome you desire, don't let things drift. Relieve the pressure with action!

Guideline # 21:
Don't Insist On Winning

To make some extra money in graduate school, I worked as a Little League umpire. That has to be one of the most frightening experiences in the world, but not because of the kids—they were great. You have to watch out for the parents! They become like wild animals that have been turned loose.

At the end of the season, I was one of the umpires chosen to work the city championship game. The game had been an excellent one. We came to the bottom of the last inning with the score tied at 3-3. There were two outs, a runner on third, and the smallest kid on the team up to bat. On the third pitch he swung and by some miracle hit the ball toward the shortstop. He headed for first; the runner on third ran for home plate; and the shortstop went for the ball. Somehow the shortstop's feet were moving faster than his body, and he tripped and fell. The runner scored—the run counted—the game was over.

As fate would have it, I turned around just in time to see this giant of a man jump up, throw his hat to the ground, and charge toward the field. (After having a parent come after me with a ball bat, I learned to be ready to move very quickly.) He by-passed me and headed toward the little shortstop, who was already visibly upset. He reached down, lifted him off the ground by his arm, and screamed, *"You lost the game! All you had to do was throw him out! What's wrong with you? We could have won it!"*

What pressure is created when winning becomes the most important thing! People who must always win enter every event filled with stress.

Guideline #22:
Be Yourself

You are the greatest person in the world when you are being yourself. You are a barrel of pressure and frustration when you are living your life from behind a mask. The number of people who spend their entire lives wearing masks is astonishing! You don't know whom you are when your life is filled with pretending.

Shakespeare knew what he was talking about when he said, *"all the world is a stage and we are simply actors."* Everyday that you let others write the script for your life, you become an actor.

It is important for you to be yourself. It is important that you write your own role and don't become someone else's creation. Wouldn't you rather be an original than a copy? The original is the real you. The copy is someone else's creation of you.

Guideline #23:
Don't Judge Yourself Too Sternly

We discussed this earlier: you are your own worst enemy. It's true in my case. When I finish a presentation, the first thing I do is take the presentation apart. Many times I am very critical of myself—sometimes too much so.

Just as others can use criticism on you, you can use it on yourself. You must constantly evaluate what you are doing and/or how well you are doing, but not to the point of self-destruction.

Have you ever listened to people talk that had nothing good to say about themselves? You must always remember that you become the product of the energy flow of your life. Don't be afraid to evaluate yourself...just make sure the end result is constructive.

Guideline #24:
Respect Yourself

Here's a question for you: *How much do you like yourself?* People respond to you in direct proportion to the way you view yourself. You view people's reactions to you in accordance with the way you see yourself.

Let me expand on something I said earlier. The way people talk about themselves tells you how they really view themselves. If you focus on your weaknesses, that's all others will be able to see of you. Other people define who you are by the picture that you paint of yourself.

Liking yourself is a prerequisite to the basic principles of growth in your life. Without self-respect, there will be no positive growth. Without self-respect, there is uncontrollable stress.

Guideline #25:
Don't Do Wrong

You have a moral definition for your life. Your ethics are the principles you use to define your understanding of right and wrong. Whenever you go against that value system, you create pressure for yourself.

Joe came to me very despondent over a meeting with his boss. Business was down and the push from management was to make sales. The boss said that the salespeople should tell clients whatever was necessary to get their orders. Joe had spoken up at that point. He said that they had never done business that way. What if they promised and could not deliver? His boss' reply was, "We'll worry about that bridge when we come to it."

Joe was upset because if he did it the boss' way he would have to go against his convictions. Once you have established a set of principles for your life, you live within them. When you go against them, you create unnecessary pressure for your life.

Guideline #26:
Don't Wait For The Sword To Fall

Have you ever lived in anticipation? You know something is going to happen or some event is going to occur. The anticipation creates pressure in your life. This pressure is not limited to events that are viewed as bad. You can be excited about something that happens and have the excitement create pressure.

If you can deal with the event or situation by speeding up the action, don't be afraid to do it. Many times you postpone action because you want to delay the end result. The postponing creates pressure. Even though you feel fear, take control. Don't sit and wait. Act and know that by acting you are controlling some of the pressure of anticipation.

What if you can't speed up the action? What do you do

with the anticipation?

First, you must understand why you have anticipation. What are your thoughts that are creating the response? Are those feelings justified or are they manufactured by the anticipation?

Second, once you've examined the reasons for your feelings, ask yourself what you can do to keep your feelings in perspective. If your feelings are out of control, it will create pressure. If you understand control, your feelings may still create pressure, but it will be pressure with some sort of understanding that makes it tolerable.

Guideline #27:
Find Security Inside You

Stress is created whenever you have to deal with insecurity. When you feel comfortable with what is going on in your life, there is a calmness about you. If you let those points of security become insecurities, they create tremendous pressure.

Jean was both a wife and a mother. She loved her life. She had a nice home, a loving husband, good children, and a very substantial income. All of these spelled security. Then, like a flash of light, it was gone.

Her husband and the children perished in a fire that destroyed their home. We spent hours together with her redefining what security means. Her tangible definition of security had been taken away from her and now her inner person had to deal with a new definition. There are many people in this world whose only definition of security is their house, their car, and their bank account—things you can taste, feel, and see. What happens if these are damaged or

129

destroyed? You find a person who must redefine security out of the insecurities that have been created.

An over-emphasis on tangible securities will cause you to place less importance on your inward security. You must learn that inward security is much more important than outward security.

Guideline #28:
Be Healthy

Your health is important. If you don't have your health, then what do you really have?

When you are out of shape, you do not handle the pressures of life very well. Your body is like a fine-tuned, high performance automobile. When it is finely tuned, it glides. When it is out of tune, it sputters and coughs and jerks and just doesn't go very far. That creates frustration and anxiety.

Your body is a complex system. For it to function at its maximum level you have to keep all the controls in order. There is so much more to being healthy than just physical fitness. To be healthy you must also be mentally and emotionally fit. Remember that your body is an integrated system.

Each part is independent, but the parts are all linked together. Being healthy means being physically fit, but it also means being emotionally in control and mentally relaxed. A total fitness program for your life is one that is designed to work on all three factors. Any program that does not emphasize all three of these aspects will leave you weak in areas that will drain the others. Life's pressures are handled more effectively through a program of total fitness.

Guideline #29:
Take One Thing At A Time

Helen was very upset with me because I was four minutes late. The appointment directly before hers had held me a few minutes longer than I had anticipated. She proceeded to tell me that her day was packed and she had places to be. Any disruption would throw her off schedule. I asked her what would happen if she didn't get things done. She got a worried look on her face and said, "Oh, I just have to get everything done today. I don't have any time left tomorrow for anything else."

Helen is typical of so many people. She didn't have time to enjoy life because of the race she was running. She was not living her life—she was only the maintenance supervisor for her own life!

You must learn that pressure is created anytime your life is going in different directions at the same time. Each event in your life requires energy. When you have a number of events draining you at the same time, it destroys your creativity and leaves you without direction. You have your own personal tug of war!

Learn that you can only correctly do one thing at a time. Direct your energy toward a project; do what needs to be done; then move onto the next project.

I watched a businesswoman once while she was working at her desk. She had six projects to finish. She would start one project then remember something about one of the other projects and start searching through the stack. You could tell she was becoming more and more frustrated.

Energy that is directed results in accomplishment. Energy that flies from one place to another results in frustration. Organize your energy according to the task. Don't allow clutter to steal your focus, drain your energy and create stacks you don't have time to deal with.

Guideline #30:
Handle Your Anger Before It Handles You

Anger is a pressure cooker about to blow its lid. Anger that isn't dealt with becomes stored-up rage with no place to vent. It's a momentary eruption resulting from trapped emotions.

Anger that is *not* controlled *will* control you! Too many people live with a storage closet inside of them. As events happen in their lives, they store the events rather than deal with them.

When there is no room left in your storage closet, you do your cleaning by exploding. You must learn that when you store emotions, you create pressure. If you could see the door to your storage closet, it might be pulsating! Your storage closet becomes an emotional depository that can and will explode at some point if it is not dealt with emotionally.

Don't store emotions! When the feelings are there, confront them. When you deal with them as they occur, you are in control of what comes out. Let them set and become attached to negative emotions and they will control you.

Guideline #31:
Find A Confidant

You are probably wondering, *"How do I learn to empty my storage closet?"* The best answer is for you to find a confidant. Everyone needs someone who will listen and will respond to him. You often store your emotions because you are either afraid to talk to someone, you are not able to talk about what is bothering you, or you have no one who will listen to you.

Pressure is created when you need to talk and you do not have the opportunity or you are afraid of the opportunity. The need to express feelings is one of the most important needs of the human race.

Society is changing its immature attitude toward seeking psychological help. People used to think that those who need psychological help were mentally sick. All of us have issues! Those who think they can handle everything by themselves are the ones with the problem. We all need a set of ears—none of us are totally self-sufficient—and many times the need is for an outsider who can serve as one who is not emotionally attached. We all need someone who will allow us to verbalize our thoughts and feelings.

For years I have been a private coach to many of the most talented people in our society. They come to me because they are struggling with a lack of understanding about their lives. They come because they are tired of opinions and are searching for solutions. They come because they are stuck in their circle of sameness and that circle is draining them daily. Many of these people have been to counselors; many have spent vast amounts of money to talk to people whose only mission is to keep them coming back.

My philosophy is this: If I can't help you find the solution within a year, I am the wrong person for you. Why a year? It takes at least four months to gain a person's trust and take their walls down; it then takes another four months to redefine most people's personal understandings about their life; finally, it takes the last four months to refocus them on the mission and establish the discipline necessary to follow through.

Find a confidant. Realize that strength is the ability to see your need for a confidant and then find that person. Weakness is knowing you need the confidant and doing nothing about finding one.

Guideline #32:
Choose Your Associates Carefully

This may sound like something your mother said to you, but it's very important in adulthood, too! Many times pressure exists because of the people that surround your life. The quality of people you decide to let into your life says a lot about the way you feel about yourself.

The #1 question I am asked is *why do I attract all the weird people to my life?*

I tell people, "I can answer the question, if you can handle the honesty. You put people in your life that are your emotional twin. Look at those around your life and they are you."

You become the product of all the things and all the people that are in your life. Most of the people around your life are a mirror of what you think and feel about you.

You must be careful not to surround yourself with people who take, but never give. You must be careful not to allow other people to be your conscience, your interpreter, or the designer of your life. Make sure that the people whom you invite into your life are those who want to participate in your growth journey. Choose these people very carefully!

Guideline #33:
Get Involved

On a sunny afternoon I was sitting on a bench and watching a young boy as he watched the rest of the children play. Wow, how he wanted to be a part of the football game . . . but he was new and didn't know how to ask. From his sideline position he would run the plays, go through all the motions of being hit, and even offer free advice on what play to run. Finally, when it seemed they were not going to ask him to play, he turned and started to walk away. I called to him and as he sat down on the bench beside me, I asked him why he didn't just ask them if he could play. He looked at me with a child's look of, "Don't you understand? They don't want me to play. I'm not a member of the club. Besides, they don't need me." I told him I really felt that they needed him. The plays he was telling them to run were better than the ones they had been running. You could see him perk up. After we talked a little more he jumped up, ran over to the group, asked to play, and became the star of the game.

I sometimes think adults are just children in taller bodies. They stand on the sidelines of life wanting to be involved, but not getting involved because of insecurities. Each person has something to offer. When you feel you can help, but are afraid to ask, you create pressure in your life.

I can't begin to tell you about the people I talk to who have so much to offer, but remain on the sidelines because:

- *They feel that they are not wanted.*
- *They don't feel like they are a part of the group.*
- *They don't know how to ask.*
- *They are afraid they will be turned down.*

135

Relieve the pressure—go for it! Believe, that because of your uniqueness, you have something to offer. Get involved!

Guideline #34:
Balance Your Work And Your Leisure

Some people spend all their waking hours working. From sun-up to sundown, work consumes all of their energy. Day after day they become less and less valuable to themselves and to those around them because they are all work and no play. They have not learned that to keep the "creative you" alive you must have diversion in your life.

One of the hardest things for many people to do is live a balanced life. It's either one extreme or the other. Many people don't see the need to go in any one particular direction until they have reached the point of exhaustion; then they try to find an alternative route.

You can control so much of the daily pressure if you look for balance. It is possible! Balance is the result of directed energy flow. It is not allowing any one area of your life to drain another. You understand that by giving energy to each area you become more creative in all areas. Whenever you take energy from one area of your life and give it to another, you create frustration in the area from which you have taken the energy. The frustration will not be dormant! It will filter its way into other areas of your life—especially into the area that is receiving the greatest amount of your energy.

Balance creates the ventilation system your life needs to handle the pressure pockets. Keep the balance! Allow the areas of your life to work together as partners, not against each other.

Remember, you are not a one-room residence; you are

four rooms and each room must support the other rooms. If there is not the support, there will not be balance. Without balance you will always be at war with yourself and the others who are part of the rooms they share with you. Balance the rooms and you can move from room to room without conflict.

Guideline #35:
Seek The Humor

There is humor in 99% of life if you would just take the time to see it! Most people cannot find the humor, because their emotional battles have taken over their life. You define the events in your life according to what that event means to you. That makes humor sometimes hard to find.

Do you understand that laughter is a pressure release? People who can laugh live under less pressure. People who can find the humor in life have a more relaxed air about them. This is not to say they are never serious, but only that they know when to release their seriousness with a point of humor.

Learn to look beyond the surface to deeper areas for your definition of the events in your life.

Humor is how we stay young. When you can't find the humor, you get old. Look at the people who don't laugh, who never seem to have fun, who are always struggling with some part of their life and see how their seriousness keeps them from enjoying life. Humor is about discovering those parts of life that create an inner smile that appears through your outer behavior.

Guideline #36:
Make Your Desires Clear

Some of your pressure is created because of

misunderstandings. Have you ever said something to someone and thought they understood exactly what you were saying, but when they explained what they understood you to say, you realized they did not understand at all? You then had a tremendous case of misunderstanding!

Understanding takes communication and very little assuming. Whenever you assume that others understand, you do not put as much energy into the communication process as you should. You make your desires clear with the energy you put into what you are saying. The terminology you use must carry common meaning to all concerned. Make your desires clear. If you expect the possibility of misunderstanding, you will do a better job of creating understanding. Think about what you want to say. If you have a point to make, be sure it is clear to you before you try to explain it to someone else. If it is not clear to you, back off and make sure your meaning will be understood before you start the communication process.

Guideline #37:
Analyze Your Pet Peeves

It's the little things in life that can be the most upsetting to you. A pet peeve is a little annoyance that can become a major disruption. Little things others do will easily upset you. You can become a reactor to other people's actions. A pet peeve is an action that creates an annoyance in your life.

You must understand what these annoyances are, why you react the way you do, and whether they deserve your energy. Many times your pet peeves do not deserve the energy you give them.

It's also true that people will use your pet peeves to gain a reaction from you. They gain pleasure from your reactions. If you do not react, they will stop. Simply not reacting to them is the easiest way to deal with the situation.

Okay, let's say you have identified a pet peeve, know why it upsets you, and have decided on an action. What do you do now? You determine whether you want to continue to deal with the annoyance or divorce yourself from the situation. You can control your reaction by controlling your mental and emotional energy. If you cannot divorce yourself from the situation or if you choose not to, you can control it by at least not dwelling on it.

Guideline #38:
Know Your Stress Level

You have to know how far you can go, how much you can tolerate, how much you can bend before you break. You are the only one who can set the boundaries for your life. It is important you know your stress level. The only place the creative part of you can develop is within the boundaries of your stress level. If you overstep the boundaries your stress will not only consume you, but it can also destroy you.

You must not work to eliminate the stress in your life; you must work to control it. In order to do that, you must know your stress level!

Guideline #39:
Correct Your Mistakes

Admit your mistakes first; that is mandatory. To really work on the pressure created by your mistakes, you must also work to correct those mistakes. A mistake is never a weakness if you are working to correct it. If a mistake is made and no effort is made to correct it, it can become a weakness.

139

Mistakes that do not receive corrective energy become habits. You know you will make mistakes. That's a part of life. Once you recognize the mistake, work to correct it.

Guideline #40:
Be Realistic

Pressure can only be controlled by those who are realistic about what's happening in their lives. It is so easy to live in a world of pretense—a world where you postpone the results of the pressure in your life, rather than control it.

Be honest about your struggles! Examine them through open eyes. Don't just see what you want to see. See what is really there, form your plan of action, and control the pressure pockets. Be realistic.

*People who work to eliminate
stress become stressful.
People who learn to control their stress
enhance their creativity.*

1.   Don't be afraid to take a risk.

2.   Turn every obstacle or problem into a creative growth experience.

3.   Make conscious decisions.

4.   Don't be afraid to make mistakes.

5.   Set priorities.

6.   If you find yourself in a rut, change your routine.

7.   Form a mental picture of the "you" who you would like to be and work on becoming that "you."

8.   Evaluate your present work or job.

9.   Keep the balance between too little and too much stress.

10. Learn to relax.

11. Don't allow criticism to stop you.

12. Work toward your dream.

13. Don't let things drift.

14. Acknowledge your fears.

15. Don't blame others.

16. Don't compromise who you are.

17. Do something for others.

18. Arrange for privacy.

19. Don't overdo a problem.

20. Make timely decisions.
21. Don't insist on winning.
22. Be yourself.
23. Don't judge yourself too sternly.
24. Respect yourself.
25. Don't do wrong.
26. Don't wait for the sword to fall.
27. Find security inside yourself.
28. Be healthy.
29. Take one thing at a time.
30. Handle your anger before it handles you.
31. Find a confidant.
32. Choose your associates carefully.
33. Get involved.
34. Balance your work and your leisure.
35. Seek the humor.
36. Make your desires clear.
37. Analyze your pet peeves.
38. Know your stress level.
39. Correct your mistakes.
40. Be realistic.

CHAPTER 11
Know Your Stress

On Tuesday, Al and I stood on the tennis court laughing, after having completed three sets of tennis. On Thursday, I stood by his hospital bed not knowing whether he would live or die.

Everything happened so fast that no one really knew what was taking place. Al was active, hard working, and seemingly in good health. Tuesday, as usual, we played tennis. Everything seemed okay, but then Al was never the type to let you know what was really going on in his life.

Thursday morning I got a call from Al's wife telling me he had suffered a heart attack and was in critical condition. All the way to the hospital, the thought kept going through my head...*what could cause a thirty-two-year-old man like Al to have a heart attack?* As far as I knew, there had been no evidence of any kind of problem.

At the hospital it seemed like an eternity before the doctor came to talk to us. He said he felt that Al was going to make it. I just had to ask the doctor why this had happened.

He looked at me and replied, *"Some time ago I tried to warn Al he needed to slow his pace and do something about the extreme pressure he was under. I told him his body was just not equipped to handle what he was asking of it. He just didn't listen."*

Some weeks later I sat in Al's hospital room and we talked about what had happened. Al was a typical young businessman; he was aggressive and wanted to get ahead.

As he told me, "Being in real estate demands that you work hard and work long hours. If I don't work hard, I don't sell houses. If I don't sell houses, I don't make money. Then, I can't provide the things for my family they want and need."

He paused, looked around, and hurtfully said, *"Look where it got me . . . all my hours of work, being away from my family, and the tension I put myself under. Look where it got me! Richard, if you ever get the chance, tell other people that it's wrong—all wrong. Success that cripples or destroys you really isn't success!"*

Al's story is a tragic example of the way many, many people live each day, placing themselves under more and more pressure. Each day they ignore the danger signals their bodies are giving them. They allow themselves to get more and more caught up in the success game. They move a little farther from reality. They forget a little more of what life is really about. Then, at some point, their health deteriorates as Al's did. They find themselves echoing his words: *"What good is it to work and work if it costs you your health and maybe even your life?"*

Many of these people continue their stress-filled lifestyles saying, "I don't plan to keep this pace forever. I only plan to do it for a little while. Then, I'm going to retire and enjoy all I have worked so hard to obtain."

What they fail to realize is that a stress-filled lifestyle is a merry-go-round. Once you hop on board and it starts to move, it is almost impossible to stop. Each revolution creates more needs; each need makes you want to stay on just a little longer. There are always the reasons and the justification for you to continue. Maybe you want to get off, but you are strapped in. Each day the merry-go-round spins faster and faster. The faster it spins, the more out of control you realize things have gotten. What does it do to you? It creates more and more pressure for you to handle.

What do you do? We've established that pressure is a normal part of life. Each day in many different ways you experience it. You deal with it at the office and at home every day.

Each day, in your personal life there is pressure. You would like to find just a few minutes for yourself; yet, when those minutes do exist, someone is always waiting to fill them.

There seems to be no stopping it. Things just spin faster and faster. The pressure builds and builds until you feel you have reached the red zone, and your body starts to scream— Danger! Danger! The reality is, the more you work to turn your pressure valve down, the more the pressure seems to build. What are you to do?

The secret has been stated time and time again throughout the pages of this book. You don't want to eliminate the pressure; you want to understand and control it. The better you understand this thing called stress the better you will understand yourself, and the better you will be able to take control away from pressure. When you are in control, pressure is your friend. When pressure is in control, it is your number one enemy.

People who work to eliminate stress become stressful; people who learn to control the stress in their lives become creative.

The effect stress will have on your life is your decision. You can spend time and energy blaming the situation, the experience, or the people, for what is happening to you.

147

Reality is — that it is your choice. You choose what and who is in control. Remember, *stress is anything in life that makes you uptight.* Anything that takes you out of your comfortable routine will place pressure on you. That pressure is not bad unless you allow it to control your life.

Controlled stress is healthy and don't let anyone tell you it isn't! It is healthy because it offers you the opportunity to be creative. That creativity will not be seen unless you take control of what is happening.

Learn the truth about stress from Al's story before you become like him. Turn your pressure valve down by learning to be the controller.

A life controlled by stress is a life that is out of control. That is the truth whether you want to accept it or not. Stress is a fact you have to handle!

This is the only life you are given. This isn't a dress rehearsal! Learn, learn, learn...about you, your stress level, your Stress House and what you must do to stop trying to eliminate your stress and start controlling it. Remember: stress out of control can kill you! The truth is that controlled stress is a positive force in your life.

REFERENCES

1. Cherry, Laurence. "On The Real Benefits of Eustress." *Psychology Today*, March 1978, p. 8

2. Ibid. p. 12-14

3. Timmermann, Tim. *Modern Stress: The Needless Killer.* unpublished, p. 16

4. Brown, Barbara. *Super Mind.* Doubleday & Company, p. 18

5. Forbes, Rosalind. *Life Stress.* Doubleday & Company, 1979, p. 98